Under a Cruel Star

A Life in Prague 1941–1968

Heda Margolius Kovály

translated from the Czech
by Franci Epstein and Helen Epstein
with the author

GRANTA

Granta Publications, 12 Addison Avenue, London W11 4QR

Published in Great Britain by Granta Books, 2012

This edition was published in the United States of America by
Plunkett Lane Press, 1986. An earlier edition of this book, together
with a political treatise by Erazim Kohak, was originally published
in Czech in Canada under the title *Na vlastní kůži* by 68 Publishers in
Toronto in 1973. That same year Horizon Press published an English
translation under the title *The Victors and the Vanquished* in New
York. A British edition of the book excluded the treatise and was
published by Weidenfeld & Nicolson under the title *I Do Not
Want to Remember*, by Heda Margolius, 1973.

Under a Cruel Star: A Life in Prague 1941–1968 is a
new translation and revised edition of the original material.

A CIP catalogue record for this book
is available from the British Library.

1 3 5 7 9 10 8 6 4 2

ISBN 978 1 84708 476 7

Printed and bound by CPI Group (UK) Ltd, Croydon, CR0 4YY

There forces carved the landscape of my life. Two of them crushed half the world. The third was very small and weak and, actually, invisible. It was a shy little bird hidden in my rib cage an inch or two above my stomach. Sometimes in the most unexpected moments the bird would wake up, lift its head, and flutter its wings in rapture. Then I too would lift my head because, for that short moment, I would know for certain that love and hope are infinitely more powerful than hate and fury, and that somewhere beyond the line of my horizon there was life indestructible, always triumphant.

The first force was Adolf Hitler; the second, Iosif Vissarionovich Stalin. They made my life a microcosm in which the history of a small country in the heart of Europe was condensed. The little bird, the third force, kept me alive to tell the story.

I carry the past inside me folded up like an accordion, like a book of picture postcards that people bring home as souvenirs from foreign cities, small and neat. But all it takes is to lift one corner of the top card for an endless snake to escape, zigzag joined to zigzag, the sign of the viper, and instantly all the pictures line up before my eyes. They linger, sharpen, and a moment of that distant past gets wedged into the works of my inner time clock. It stops, skips a beat, and loses part of the irreplaceable, irretrievable present.

The mass deportation of Jews from Prague began two years after the outbreak of the war, in the fall of 1941. Our transport left in October and we had no idea of our destination. The order

5

was to report to the Exposition Hall, to bring food for several days and essential baggage. No more.

When I got up that morning, my mother turned to me from the window and said, like a child, "Look, it's almost dawn. And I thought the sun would not even want to rise today."

The inside of the Exposition Hall was like a medieval madhouse. All but the steadiest nerves were on the point of snapping. Several people who were seriously ill and had been brought there on stretchers died on the spot. A Mrs. Tausig went completely crazy, tore her false teeth out of her mouth, and threw them at our lord and master, Obersturmbannfuehrer Fiedler. There were babies and small children who cried incessantly and, just beside my parents, a small fat bald man sat on his suitcase playing his violin as if none of the surrounding bedlam were any concern of his. He played Beethoven's Concerto in D Major, practicing the same passages over and over again.

I wandered around among those thousands of people looking for familiar faces. That was how I first happened to see him. To this day, I believe he was the most handsome man I have ever seen. He was sitting, calm and erect, on a black trunk with silver brackets, wearing a black suit, a white shirt, a gray tie, and a black overcoat topped by a black homburg. He had gray eyes and a perfectly trimmed gray moustache. His slim, delicate hands were folded on the handle of an umbrella rolled up as thin as a toothpick. In the middle of that chaos, among all those people dressed in sweaters, heavy boots, and ski jackets, he looked as incongruous as if he were sitting there naked.

Startled, I stopped, and he rose. With a slight bow and a smile, he offered me a seat beside him on his trunk. He was a professor of classical philology from Vienna. After the Nazis had annexed Austria, he had found refuge in Prague, and there the Germans had caught up with him. When I asked why he had not dressed in a more practical way for such a journey into the unknown, he answered that he always dressed in the same way and disliked the idea of changing his habits under the pressure of circumstances. In any event, he said, he considered it most important to maintain

6

equanimity *rebus in arduis*. Then he began talking about classical literature and ancient Rome. I listened with rapt attention. From that time on I sought him out whenever I had the opportunity, and he always welcomed me with his courteous smile and, it seemed, with pleasure.

Two days later, we boarded the train. Even though in the following years I would experience infinitely more grueling transports, this one seemed to be the worst because it was the first. If every beginning is hard, the beginning of hardship is the hardest. We were not yet inured to sounds of gunshots followed by agonizing screams, to unendurable thirst, nor to the suffocating air in the crammed cattle cars.

Upon our arrival in Lodz, we were greeted by a snowstorm. It was only October, but in the three years I spent there I never again saw such a blizzard. We left the railroad station, plodding with difficulty against the wind and, for the first time, saw people who were dying of hunger, little children almost naked and barefoot in the snow.

A few days later, I wandered into a basement. The young people from our transport were sitting on the floor around a kerosene lamp and someone was playing Czech folk songs on a harmonica. There was an arched ceiling on which the lamp cast long strangely shaped shadows, making it look like the vault of a cathedral. I stood in the doorway and thought: now an angel should appear and leave a mark of blood on the forehead of everyone who will die here.

The concentration camp of Lodz, officially called the Litzmannstadt Ghetto, was really part of the outskirts of the city, a dilapidated slum enclosed by a wall that was made of wooden boards and barbed wire. For some time after our arrival, people in our transport stayed together in one of the few undamaged buildings of the ghetto, and I could still see my professor once in a while. Some weeks later, another transport arrived and we received orders to move. We scattered into the decaying tenements already populated by close to one hundred thousand Polish Jews living in unimaginable conditions, and we lost track of one another.

One of the people in our transport was our family doctor, a splendid old gentleman, who had known me since birth. He was now more than seventy years old, but every day he would go out into the narrow streets of the ghetto, walking at an even pace, cane in hand, searching for those who needed his help. Medications were in pitifully short supply, but he would say that often just the appearance of a doctor would make a patient feel a little better. I was glad when he accepted my offer to help him. The two of us wandered together from one hovel to the next, climbing thousands of stairs, often unable to offer the sick more than the comfort of a few kind words. Frequently, I had to bring in a pail of water first and wash and tidy up around the patient before the doctor could examine him.

One day we entered an almost bare but spotlessly scrubbed room where a child lay on a heap of rags, a little boy of four, just a small skeleton with huge eyes. His mother, so thin that she herself looked like a child, was crying quietly in the corner. The doctor took out his stethoscope, listened for a while, patted the little boy's head and sighed; he could do no more. At that moment, the child turned toward his mother and sternly, like an adult, said, "You see Mother? I told you all the time I was hungry but you didn't give me anything to eat. And now I'm going to die."

As we left the house, we were stopped by an elderly woman who asked us to call in at the next building. There was a sick man there, she said, who had not been seen for several days. The building was deserted, split in two from the roof all the way down to the cellar, and looked on the verge of collapse. It took some time before we found the one room which still had a door. We knocked, but there was no answer. Then the doctor opened the door, and we walked in. A torn mattress lay on the narrow strip of floor. There was a pile of dirty rags and refuse in one corner; next to the mattress was a suitcase half-filled with books. Lying on the mattress was a dead man, his body swarming with a myriad of fat white lice. They also crawled over the face of the Venus de Milo, who smiled serenely from a page of the open book on the man's chest. The book had dropped from his hand as he lay dying.

I leaned over him. It was my professor.

The doctor said, "He's only been dead a few hours."

About a year later, at work, I heard the bell of the ghetto's one fire engine. Although this was nearly a daily occurrence at the time, I somehow knew that the fire was at the house where I was living. It was strictly forbidden to leave a place of work, but I sneaked out and ran along the walls toward the half-ruin where we were housed. I arrived breathless to find only my mother, throwing some essentials into a suitcase. My father came running a moment later and, although he had already grown quite weak by that time, began darting back and forth trying to help. My cousin Jindrisek was lying motionless in a heap, nailed to the floor by tuberculosis of almost every organ in his body. His black hopeless eyes followed our every move. Firemen surrounded the house. There was lots of smoke and screaming. The cold was bitter and the water did not run, but people did not panic. Even then, resignation prevailed. I remember how, with my father, I dragged out two suitcases, sat my mother down on them wrapped in blankets, and how I returned to the house to get Jindrisek.

The firemen would not let me back in. One of them swung at me with his stick and, while my father tried to stop him, I slipped back inside. Jindrisek tried to get up but could not. I started yelling at him, fiercely, desperately. I pulled his arm up around my neck—he was terribly heavy for someone made up only of skin and bones—and I dragged him outside, shouting at him all the while, trying to infuse him with my will, my energy. Over the threshold. Across the yard. Across the street. He sagged with every step but we got there and he fell, exhausted, onto another suitcase. My mother covered him and put his head in her lap. My father and I stood beside them and I hid my face on my father's shoulder.

The fire was finally brought under control, and we dragged the suitcases back into the house. Now people began to help one another, all of us exhausted from the exertion and the excitement. After everything was back in place, I put a big pot of water on to heat. Jindrisek was lying on the floor with his face to the wall, his eyes closed, a slight smile on his face. Slowly I undressed, scrubbed myself clean, combed my hair, dressed, polished my shoes, and then went unhurriedly back to work.

Jindrisek died about three weeks later. When I returned home one evening, my mother told me in a whisper that he had asked her to sing the Czech national anthem, "Where is my home?" and a folk song called "Where have all my young days gone?" I sat down beside him on the floor. He was in a coma. I tried to force spoonfuls of food into his mouth and, although he was unconscious, his craving for food was so strong that he clenched his teeth around the spoon. It required some effort on my part to free it. I slipped my hands under his head and back and held him. He stopped breathing minutes later.

My mother prayed, but I could not see the point of pleading with God for someone who had to die at the age of sixteen after so much suffering. There is nothing more senseless, more cruel, than dying before we have become guilty of sins that might justify death. For a long time afterward, I felt as though those black yearning eyes were watching me from Jindrisek's corner of the room.

It seems to me, sometimes, when people say that everything passes, that they don't know what they are saying. The real past is what Jindrisek was thinking as he lay there in his corner on the floor and watched me walk out into the sun and the cold. It is what went through my mother's mind as she sang "Where is my home?" to her dying nephew behind barbed wire in the Lodz Ghetto. The real past is enclosed in itself and leaves no memory behind.

It seems beyond belief that in Czechoslovakia after the Communist coup in 1948, people were once again beaten and tortured by the police, that prison camps existed and we did not know, and that if anyone had told us the truth we would have refused to believe it. When these facts were discussed on foreign broadcasts, over Radio Free Europe or the BBC, we thought it only more proof of the way the "imperialists" lied about us. It took the full impact of the Stalinist terror of the 1950s to open our eyes.

It is not hard for a totalitarian regime to keep people ignorant. Once you relinquish your freedom for the sake of "understood necessity," for Party discipline, for conformity with the regime, for the greatness and glory of the Fatherland, or for any of the substitutes that are so convincingly offered, you cede your claim to the truth. Slowly, drop by drop, your life begins to ooze away just as surely as if you had slashed your wrists; you have voluntarily condemned yourself to helplessness.

In the last of the concentration camps that held me during the war, we worked in a brickyard, far from the camp. It was late autumn, beautiful but cold. In the mornings when we stood for roll call long before dawn, a thick crust of hoarfrost covered the ground. It would not thaw until afternoon. We wore nothing but short shifts made of burlap, no shoes, no underwear. We used to collect the scraps of paper that were strewn about our workplace, especially the heavy cement bags that were thrown out. Even though it was strictly forbidden, we stuffed them under our shifts so that we would freeze a little less. The morning roll call lasted two hours. Then we marched to a funny little train made up of flatcars, each holding two long benches mounted on a wooden floor. The trip to work took one hour. Then there was a half-hour hike to the factory, twelve hours of passing along bricks, the trip back to camp, another roll call, a little turnip soup, a slice of bread, and a short restless night.

The trip on the train was the worst thing about it all for most of the girls. During that hour we became so chilled that when we finally reached our destination, we fell rather than stepped off the train. It took us half the day to warm up a little. But I loved those trips. The tracks crossed an area under which an entire industrial complex had been built. Clouds of steam issued out from the earth in many places; mysterious iron constructions and fantastic twisted pipes rose from the moss-covered ground of the woods. The sun was already rising and, since there was always a thick fog hugging the ground, the sun's rays broke through it and colored the mist a variety of deep pinks, an orange, gold and blue. Out of this shimmering vapor, dark shapes of trees and bushes emerged, drifted toward us, and vanished again. Several clusters of trees seemed especially beautiful to me, and I always looked out for them. I remember, even now, a small uprooted spruce resting on a mound while another handsome symmetrical one stood above it straight and solemn, as if standing guard over the body of a fallen comrade.

Sunday was designated for work in the camp, but most often, we worked without food because our camp kommandant had calculated that even so cheap a thing as a turnip when multiplied by one thousand could bring a nice sum on the black market. We fasted on most Sundays as a result, until the management of the enterprise we worked for complained that the work force was fainting on Mondays and was not cost-efficient.

The owner of the brickyard where about fifty of us worked was an odd fellow. He must have been of Russian or German-Russian origin, skinny, with a shock of white hair, and he always wore a black belted Russian shirt. He would say, over and over again to our great amusement, that if we did not work hard and help the Reich to victory, the Russians would come and murder us all.

One Monday a trainload of coal arrived at the brickyard and the order was given to unload it, on the double. The chunks of coal were huge, mixed with stones, and very few of us had enough strength to lift our shovels. After a few hours, most of the girls were stretched out on the piles of coal, exhausted, nearly unconscious. At that moment, our boss appeared and began to shout: What kind of workers were we that we didn't even know how to handle a shovel? For the money he paid us, all we ever did was loll around!

I don't know what came over me then. The fast must have softened my brain. I threw down my shovel and screamed back at him: How dare he yell at us? Almost all of us were students, educated women. If he expected us to perform hard labor, why didn't he see to it that we were fed properly and treated as laborers? The girl lying on the coal pile nearest me grabbed my ankles and tried to pull me down, but I went right on screaming as if I had lost my senses. The boss stared at me but did not pull his gun or call the guards. To everyone's amazement, he turned around and left. The rest of the day passed in great trepidation as we all waited for the consequences of my madness. But nothing happened.

The next morning he appeared as soon as we had picked up our shovels and asked: *Wo ist die Studentin?* My anger had long since cooled and I was stiff with fear as he led me away into the brickyard. But that strange man only announced to me in a dry and rather polite tone that, from that day on, I would be working at the kiln bringing in the coal from outside in a wheelbarrow and stoking the fire. It was the cherished dream of every inmate of a concentration camp to work under a roof where it was warm. However, this was labor for two strong men and I could not possibly have handled it had it not been for the workers inside, French prisoners-of-war, good fellows who helped me and who, in fact, often did a good deal of my work.

13

One afternoon, toward evening, the boss appeared with two Frenchmen and ordered them to help me bring in a supply of coal. He returned about an hour later, sent them out, asked me to sit down beside him on a stone ledge in the wall of the kiln and said only: Tell me.

As long as I live I shall not forget that dark cave-like place, the black walls streaked with the reflection of flames, the old man dressed in black who listened and listened and seemed to wither, to shrink before my eyes as if, with each of my sentences, part of him faded. Only once again was I to have a similar experience— with my own child, when I finally dared tell him how his father died.

I told the old man in the Russian shirt about the ghetto in Lodz where the cesspool cleaners had whistled Beethoven as they worked and where close to one hundred thousand people had been murdered or had died of starvation. I told him how the trains would arrive from Polish villages bringing men with bloody heads and women wrapped in shawls and how, once the trains were gone, the women undid their wraps and pulled out their babies, some of them dead by suffocation but a few still alive, saved from German bayonets. I told him how, a few months later, the SS would arrive and throw those same babies into trucks and cart them off to the gas chambers. I talked about the public executions, about hangings where the bodies were left on the gallows for weeks while we walked by, about the carloads of bloody clothing that we tore into strips and wove into mats for German tanks so that the soldiers could keep their feet warm. How, when the battlefront had come into earshot of our camp, a German colonel bedecked with gold braid had arrived, assembled all of us, and proclaimed: "We have to evacuate the ghetto now but do not be afraid. I give you my word of honor as a German officer that no harm will come to you. You will be well cared for . . . " and how, one week later, those who had survived the transport in sealed cattle cars walked through the gates of the electrified wire fence, straight into the black smoke of Auschwitz.

By then, I had forgotten where I was and who I was talking to.

14

I saw the Auschwitz block again, the barracks that had been horse stables crowded with a thousand half-crazed girls shaved bald, who howled under the whips like a pack of wolves. The guards, just as demented in their fury as the prisoners in their pain and terror, ran up and down the center aisle of the block, lashing out in blind rage at the girls in the stalls. And above all this, Mrs. Steinova from Prague stood on a platform, shaven bare like the rest of us, singing the aria "The moonlight on my golden hair" from Dvorak's opera *Rusalka* by order of the block Kommandant who had decided the mood on her block should be cheerful.

I saw myself as we knelt for a whole day and night, our knees scraped raw against the sandy ground, propping up the girls who fainted because we knew that whoever collapsed would never get up again. That was the time one of the girls had tried to escape. All of Auschwitz had to kneel until they captured her and when they did, they called a roll call, broke her arms and legs while we watched and only then dragged her off to the gas.

But I did not say much about Auschwitz. Human speech can only express what the mind can hold. You cannot describe hammer blows that crush your brain. Instead, I gave the old man a detailed account of the kind of life we led in the camp from which we arrived every morning in his brickyard. I also told him that there had been girls with us who had arrived directly from home and that a few dozen of them were pregnant. One evening they had all been summoned to the main barracks and we never saw them again. The following morning, a special detail was ordered to clean puddles of blood from the barracks floor.

I do not remember what else I told him. I only know that he did not say a word for as long as I spoke and, when I heard the shouting of orders outside that meant we were returning to camp and got up to leave, he remained sitting, hunched into himself, his head in his palms.

That man lived in Nazi Germany and had daily contact with a concentration camp and its inmates, yet he knew nothing. I am quite sure he did not. He had simply thought that we were convicts, sentenced by a regular court of law for proven crimes.

P eople often ask me: How did you manage? To survive the
camps! To escape! Everyone assumes it is easy to die but
that the struggle to live requires a superhuman effort. Mostly, it
is the other way around. There is, perhaps, nothing harder than
waiting passively for death. Staying alive is simple and natural and
does not require any particular resolve.

The idea of escape began, I think, back when our guard Franz
shot yet another girl. At the time we had already been marching
for a few weeks. The Eastern front had come so close to our camp
that we could hear the rumbling of battle. The camp had to be
evacuated. Our guard was reinforced; we received civilian coats—
taken, we found out later, from people killed in the gas chambers—
and an extra allotment of bread. Then we set out on foot, under
twice the usual number of bayonets, toward the west, out of Poland
into Germany.

Our column plodded along, inching its way across the frozen
snow. Only a few of us had the strength left to turn our heads and
look back as we heard the occasional shot from behind. Redheaded
Franz kept close to little Eva from dawn to dusk, taking fatherly
care of her, scrounging up food for her, full of affable concern.
He turned around only now and then, mostly whenever the column
rounded a convenient curve, and fired his gun into the rear where
there were always a few stragglers. Whenever he scored a hit, he

ran back along with another of our guards. Then the two of them would dig and scrape for a while in the ditch by the side of the road. Franz would then hurry back to fawn over the terrified Eva, who was only fifteen and would sob whole nights through.

During all these days and weeks of marching, I walked next to Hanka, my head bent, looking at our bare feet sinking into the slush. We talked only a little, softly, and only about one thing: escape. Just as Franz fired the last shot of his that I remember, we passed a crudely-lettered sign which read TO PRAGUE. We slowed down, pressed each other's hands, and exchanged a solemn and somewhat ridiculous promise not to deviate from that direction. Whatever happened, we would reach Prague. From the moment we had left the camp behind and with it the crackling of gunshots as the SS finished off the girls in the hospital barracks, we had thought of nothing else but escape. Many of the others were thinking the same thing; some even made small attempts. Somewhere along the way, they would slip into the bushes and let the whole column pass by. But then they would always rejoin us. It was just too difficult to face the unknown alone.

"You see," Hanka said, "as long as we march like this, all together, there's nothing we can do but walk and walk and wait until Franz guns us down somewhere. We can't reproach ourselves for anything, and nobody can expect us to do more. But once we're free, everything will be up to us. Then we'll have to act."

She was right I thought. As long as we marched together, we had the comfort of belonging. We all shivered and starved and were abused together. We shared a common destiny, a common journey, and at the end of that journey, maybe even the same death. But should we free ourselves. . . . At that moment, I understood—one single act would be enough. All it would take was one decision and I would reach the greatest freedom that anyone at that time and place on earth could possibly have. Once I slipped out from under the bayonets, I would be standing outside the system. I would not belong anywhere or to anything. No one would know of my existence. Perhaps I would only gain a few days or a few hours, but it would be a freedom that millions of people could

17

not even imagine. No prohibitions, no orders would be of concern to me. Should I be caught, I would be like a bird shot in flight, like the wind caught in a sail.

Usually we slept under the open sky but that night we stopped in a village. First we stood on the village green where we were watched by curious eyes peeping out from every window, and then later alongside a wall that ran around a large farm. Finally, we marched through a gate of that wall into a vast yard, then through a smaller gate of a picket fence, and we came into an inner yard enclosing a huge barn. Hanka shrugged her shoulders and said, "Well that's that. Our worries are over for tonight—not even a mouse could get out of here. A barn door, a fence, and a wall!"

We stamped our feet in the mud for a long while, waiting for our dinner. The villagers provided it from their own stockpiles: two warm potatoes for each of us. Then came the rush into the barn and a fight for a sleeping place where it was least likely that someone would, in the pitch dark, step on your face with a wooden clog.

For a moment, I lingered by the gate of the barn. Surely by morning there would be no one awake to watch us. The guards would take naps as they always did whenever we could be locked in somewhere. The lock hanging by two rusty nails on the barn door was an ordinary padlock.

"Listen!" One of the girls grabbed my hand and pulled me into the shadows behind the door. "I heard we're turning north tomorrow. We'll never be as close as today."

So it seemed that everybody knew what was on my mind!

"And look what I found: a pair of shoes! They don't match and the tops are only tied to the soles with wire but they're better than nothing."

I hid the shoes under my coat. Then I took another look at the lock. Since I owned the greatest treasure a prisoner could have— a knife—and had been guarding it all these months for an occasion such as this, I thought I had better pull out one nail right away. Hanka and I whispered together for a while before we fell asleep, but the leap into freedom still seemed too steep. It demanded a clear decision; we had grown unaccustomed to thinking clearly and had almost forgotten how to make decisions. We fell asleep in the middle of a sentence, without a plan.

I woke up with a start, with the feeling that I was going to miss something crucial. I had to do something very important in a hurry—oh yes! There was darkness all around me, and the rustle of straw. From time to time, a slight moan, as though a large tired animal was turning and stretching in the dark. The slits in the barnboards were paling. Soon it would be dawn. I shook the knee that dug into my ribs from the right. "Hanka!" I said. "Let's go!"

Hanka woke up right away and understood what I was saying but she could not get a grip on herself. "I'm just so cold," she said, and started to crawl back under the straw.

"Hanka, I'm going," I whispered. "If you want, follow me. But make it fast."

At the door, I twisted out the second nail and was out. The guard on duty was still snoring somewhere. A premonition of light had already tinged the darkness; daybreak was very near.

I tied a piece of cloth over my stubby head that had been shaved bald as a knee only six months earlier in Auschwitz. Then I started picking blades of straw off my coat, but still no one came. At long last, the door opened and Hanka ran out. I did not leave her any time to change her mind. I climbed over the fence and ran across the yard to where the outer wall was crumbling and could easily be scaled. Before I could get up from my knees on the other side, Hanka landed beside me. We scrambled up and had not yet reached the corner where the wall turned when another head appeared. It was Zuzka, who whispered hoarsely, "Mana and Andula are right behind me."

The three of us squeezed into a recess in the wall of the next farm. Mana came running toward us. As we saw her we heard a gunshot; Andula did not make it.

We cowered in our little nook, trembling so hard it was almost audible, and someone said, "Let's go back."

"Nonsense. Once you're out, you're not going to crawl back, are you? They're in a big mess now. First the old man's going to give them hell for slaughtering a girl in the middle of the village—you know he doesn't like that kind of thing—and then they'll have to have a roll call. Before they count everybody and think of a way to explain why four of us are missing, we have to be miles away."

That sounded logical and we calmed down. The sun was rising. From where we stood, we had a good view of the flat landscape which rose in a slight wave on the horizon. There was not much snow, just earth and bare trees. It was a landscape as open as the palm of a hand, with no forest, no sign of a hiding place. In the distance we could see columns of men flanked by bands of soldiers, probably prisoners-of-war.

Just then, from around the corner of the wall, appeared a skinny little girl of about twelve holding two large slices of bread.

"Don't be afraid of me," she said in Czech. "I know who you are."

When I recovered from shock, I stammered in panic, "Little girl, for God's sake, you must not talk to us. Go home! Run!"

The little girl only smiled and pushed the bread into Mana's hand.

"Take it," she said. "We have plenty. And I'll lead you out of here. I'm sure you want to go home and don't know how."

"Run along! What would your mother say? Run!"

But the child only glanced over to her side where an older woman, her head wrapped in a scarf, was standing nodding.

"That's my mother! She sent me. We're also Czechs, you know."

We stared at her in amazement for a moment, but then set about ripping off the striped squares of cloth from the backs of one another's coats, the squares that marked us as concentration camp inmates. Seconds later, we were on our way, running after the little girl across a field. It was high time.

By then the countryside was wide awake. Fortunately for us, the roads were crowded. Wagons piled high with evacuated families and their household implements lumbered slowly by, along-side detachments of prisoners under guard and local people hurrying to work. Some of them turned to look at us but we walked rapidly, our eyes to the ground. Our temples pulsed with the beat of an almost insane joy. Free at last! No bayonets! No electrified or barbed wire!

Hanka was once again walking beside me, musing, "You know, there's just one thing about this situation that bothers me: the fact that, right now, we exist totally outside of the law."

I looked at her and exploded with laughter. I laughed until I wept. I laughed as I had not laughed in at least five years.

I t was getting dark. Our little girl had left us long ago, with a lot of useful advice as a farewell—which way to go, where to find reliable people, whom to avoid. Thanks to her we made it to the demarcation line that separated the German Reich from the truncated territory of the former Czechoslovak Republic, now called the Protectorate of Bohemia and Moravia. The Protectorate had been occupied by the Germans since 1939.

Hungry and exhausted, we barely dragged ourselves along, chilled to the bone by the wind blowing through our rags. But those first few hours of freedom had changed us a great deal. The apathetic, worn-out shadows who had made an escape out of sheer hopelessness were now gripped by a fierce will to live. It was no longer enough for us to spite death with a few extra hours or days of freedom. Now we began to believe we had found the road back to life. Fear and hope drove us down this narrow path that unwieldy common sense would never have dared to take; fear and hope had saved us so often in the years when there was so little opportunity for courage or ingenuity.

The road turned and began to slope into a valley toward a village with a large factory. We stopped a little boy and asked, "Where does Mr. Cermak live?"

"There is no Mr. Cermak here."

"I must have gotten his name wrong then. He's Czech. Are there any Czechs you know who live here?"

22

"There are no Czechs here," said the little boy.

What now? We retreated into the bushes by the side of the road for a conference. There was the blast of a siren: the shift at the local factory was over and a group of women, workers there, began to come toward us on the road. We could hear them talking in the distance. Poles! We stayed in our hide-out until we saw one woman walking alone. She looked tired but not much older than us. Zuzka got up her courage and crawled out of the bushes: *"Prosze pani. . . . "*

Without hesitation, the woman invited us to her home. She lived a little bit farther down the road in a miserable, run-down cottage. Her little girl was already standing in the doorway waiting. As soon as we sat down we began telling her the tale we had concocted on the way: that we had been in Germany, assigned to a work camp, that there had been an air-raid during which all our possessions and documents had been destroyed and that now we were trying to get back home. Finally, one of us dared to blurt out what we needed to know: How could we cross the demarcation line?

The young Polish woman listened to us in silence. Did she believe anything we were telling her? It was hard to say. But she had a suggestion: There was a Czech woman living at the far end of the village who might be able to help. We should wait until dark and then she would take us there.

Silently, on tiptoe almost, we hurried along the whole length of the sprawling village. Our guide knocked on the closed shutter of a cottage that gleamed white in the darkness. A resolute female voice answered and, after a few whispers, the door opened. We realized by the speed at which our Polish friend disappeared that she had not believed one word of our story and had been well aware of the dangers of accompanying us.

Plump and energetic, Mrs. Nemcova did not wait for us to explain anything. She seated us in her sparkling-clean kitchen around a table covered with a white tablecloth and placed a loaf of bread in the center. Clenching our teeth, we bit into that bread with our eyes. Surely, we thought, this could only be a symbol of hospitality. Who, in the middle of a war, could afford to give away a loaf of bread? But Mrs. Nemcova took out a knife and cut off so large a slab for each of us that half the loaf disappeared. At that moment, everything faded, the whole world stood aside. There was nothing alive in the whole universe but the four of us and that huge, sweet-smelling, wonderful loaf of bread.

Mrs. Nemcova had obviously had some experience with people like us. She knew of a border crossing and told us that, as a matter of fact, the evening we had chosen would be a convenient time to cross because there was a party planned at the local pub. By ten o'clock all the policemen would be drunk. At ten-thirty, we sneaked out of her house. Not a light flickered anywhere. We could hear distant music, voices, the barking of dogs.

Mrs. Nemcova took me by one hand and Hanka by the other. Zuzka and Mana followed close behind. She led us around dark-ened houses and quiet, bare gardens out into the fields. We took our shoes off so that we would not lose them in the dark and ran barefoot across the frozen ground. I heard Hanka's quiet sobs and Mrs. Nemcova's whispered encouragements. We ran, more and more frantically and, just when it seemed that we were incapable of another step, Mrs. Nemcova said, "Here you are: home. You don't have to run as fast anymore but don't dawdle. At the crossing there's a good watchman—you don't have to be afraid of him. But watch out for the next village. There the police have dogs."

We embraced her and ran on, alone again. Hanka complained that she couldn't keep going but I dragged her along, almost crush-ing her hand, whispering, "Hang in there! Even if we have to crawl on all fours we'll make it home."

We reached the checkpoint at last. Just as we crawled under the barrier, the door of the guardhouse opened and a cranky voice mumbled, "Well women, any of you have any cigarettes to spare?" It was only when we were quite a bit farther along that we allowed ourselves to slow down. We decided to make a detour around the village with the police dogs. Zuzka, whose home was in a nearby town, now announced with a flourish that she would provide shelter for us all. She was the daughter of a mixed marriage, and some of her relatives had not been deported. Soon we would come to an area where she knew her way around and, with luck, we would reach her town before daybreak.

Gratefully, patiently, we crept through a silence full of sounds, a darkness full of shadows. For the first time since I had woken up that morning, I started to breathe easily. I still was alert to every rustle and kept probing the darkness for danger, but something inside me began to loosen up. It seemed to me that I was holding my fragile freedom cupped in my hands. What would I make of it? I might lose it very soon. There was no time to waste. I did not even dare think what I would do when I got to Prague. I did not know whether I would even get there. But my life was no longer broken in two. Suddenly there was continuity. I was no longer a camp inmate, a victim destined for destruction, but a human being, a woman with a past and a future.

The step that lay before us, the transition from the freedom of a bird to the freedom among people proved to be the most difficult part of our journey. We had to find home again, to find the place where we belonged, and, for that, the simple fact of return was not enough. I think sometimes that the road which, years later, led us into another disaster began with this very step. For many people in Czechoslovakia after the war, the Communist revolution was just another attempt to find the way home, to fight their way back to humanity.

But on that first day back, everything seemed promising. We arrived in Zuzka's town before dawn, and her relatives welcomed us with great joy. They found a place for Mana to stay for a while and even produced a nice elderly man to drive Hanka and me most of the way to Prague in his truck. He dropped us off only a few miles away from the last stop of the city streetcar. We were all right until we boarded it. Then, once again, we were paralyzed by fear.

This was the sixth year of the German occupation. Thousands of people had been shot, whole villages had been wiped out, just for helping the Resistance or for harboring escaped prisoners. If the Gestapo caught us, it meant death not only for us but for anyone who helped us or was even casually associated with us.

Just to see an "illegal" without reporting him to the police was, at the time, a capital crime. The police were continually searching homes, checking identity papers, prowling the streets. Certainly there were people who would recognize us. Many things must have changed in our absence; there had to be new regulations we knew nothing about. We could give ourselves away at any moment. If anyone just took a good look at us he would see the imprint of the camps in our faces; he would realize right away who we were.

The streetcar rumbled into downtown Prague. When it stopped in the center of the city, Hanka looked at me silently, squeezed my elbow and stepped off. I was left alone in the car full of people but they did not seem to notice me. They all had their own lives and their own wartime concerns. Nothing, perhaps, as horrible as what we had been through, but all suffering can become intolerable. Maybe some of them were as worn out by running into shelters and standing on lines for food as we were by the terrors of the camps.

During those years Prague had changed, perhaps even more than I had. Most of my friends and relatives were still in concentration camps and I would have had no idea where to turn had it not been for Jenda. Jenda, who was my closest friend, could only have changed for the better. I knew that if he was still alive and free, I would be safe. The day before our deportation, he had come to our home with a small gift for everyone and had declared, "Whatever happens, I'll be your anchor. If you can, send me your messages. Should you be separated, count on meeting again at my place. If anything happens to me, I'll find a replacement. I'll never stop waiting for you to come back. You'll always have somewhere to come back to."

It was already evening when I reached the apartment house where Jenda lived and, as I slowly walked up the stairs, my feet hurt. Somehow it was difficult to walk. I arranged my scarf around my head and rang the bell. The door opened. It was Jenda—what luck!

He did not seem to recognize me. No wonder, I thought. I tried a smile but, at that instant, his eyes flashed with such terrible shock and with such horror that my smile fell away. Jenda grabbed my hand, glanced down at the stairwell, and pulled me inside. He closed the door behind us and then blurted out, "For God's sake, what brings you here?"

The answer stuck in my throat. So this was my anchor, this terrified, trembling wretch who could not even look me straight in the eye. Was this really Jenda? I looked around the room, trying to latch onto something familiar, something intimate. There was his bookcase. The easy chair by the window. Things old and familiar. But there was also a new red carpet, a new phonograph, and a few paintings I had not seen before.

We faced each other silently. Then he spoke. I did not let him go on with his explanations for too long; things were clear without the talk. I saw that he felt ashamed of himself and guilty, but that his fear was stronger than anything else. All he could think of was the deadly danger that had walked in with me: Was I sure no one had seen me on the stairs? He wanted not to know me, to know nothing about me and live. Live in peace and quiet in the middle of death and desperation. Still, I believe that while he was talking to me he realized that his calm was gone for good. Even if he were never to hear from me again, his life would not be the same.

I went out into the street again. It was dark and almost deserted. One of my parents' old friends lived nearby, a woman I had always called Auntie. Before our deportation she had hidden away some of my clothing and other things that would now prove useful. Perhaps she would let me stay the night.

The moment I rang the bell, I heard slippered feet shuffling nervously down the hall. I must have scared her; she had learned to be wary of visitors. But as it turned out, she was a courageous old woman and, after recovering from her initial shock, she welcomed me warmly, settling me down on her velvet sofa beneath a wall covered with family photographs.

"Let me stay the night Auntie? Tomorrow I'll find something."

She nodded, her eyes brimming with tears. Then she started moving through her apartment, scrounging up whatever she could find for me. She went through closets and drawers and finally came up with a complete set of clothing from before the war which would make me inconspicuous in the street. Then she tucked me under a plaid blanket and sat down on a chair near the door with her hands folded in her lap. She sat there the whole night through without shutting an eye, as if her vigil could save us from danger.

It was still dark when I walked back out into the street. I felt good in my clean change of clothes and after a big breakfast but I realized that my situation had taken a turn for the worse. Until then, I had had to face only the police system of a fascist regime. Now I had to cope with a worse enemy, human fear and indifference. Until the day before, I had kept in my mind one goal—to reach Prague and to find Jenda. Now I was looking for a human being whose humanity would prove greater than his fear.

I walked the streets waiting for daylight before I dared call on another old friend, Franta. Even if he himself could not help me, I could at least find out from him what had happened to my other friends. Franta had always been an ambitious, responsible young man who had worked his way through school while supporting his widowed mother. He had slaved away from morning till night, worked on farms while the rest of us took vacations, tutored students during the school year and took on the hardest jobs just to earn some extra money. He never doubted his capabilities or questioned his goals. The war, I thought, must have wrecked his plans too.

Franta opened his door in a sweatsuit, still unshaved. He stared at me for a moment, then stepped back, and let me into the hall.

"Franta, I ran away from the camp. I need help. Do you know where I could hide for a couple of days? Where I could rest? Do you know anyone with contacts in the Resistance? The war's almost over. It's a matter of months."

In the darkness of the hall I could not see Franta's face, and he did not say a word. Then he opened the nearest door and said, "Come in. Sit down."

For a while he paced nervously around the room. Then he sat down facing me, took out a cigarette, looked at it, put it down on the table, picked it up, finally lit it.

28

"I need to look at you," he said. "I have to get a really good look at a person who escapes from a concentration camp, walks around Prague without any identity papers, has no place to sleep, and still thinks she can stay alive. That's really exciting. I myself have been trying to gain a sense of personal freedom ever since the beginning of the Occupation—even for a few moments. One hour of it. I haven't succeeded yet. It's impossible. You liberate yourself from direct oppression and you sink into something even worse. You have to run and hide and in the end you get caught anyway. Forgive me, but I can't imagine how you can save yourself. You clearly did what you thought best in your situation but it goes against all reason. Look, I could pretend that I'm going to try and help you. I could make promises and lie. But it would be no good. If you look at it rationally, you'll see it's hopeless."

I got up and walked to the door. Franta jumped up to stop me.

"Please don't leave yet," he said. "I've struggled with these questions endlessly. When and how should one risk one's life? You escaped because you were probably convinced you'd be killed. But, in my opinion, the chances that you'll lose your life are much greater this way than if you had stayed in camp. After all, some people will survive even there. You have much less hope in this situation. And am I justified in risking my or anyone else's life for something I consider a lost cause? What sense does it make anyway to risk one life for another?"

I stepped back to try to look him in the eye, and Franta threw his cigarette into an ashtray. After another moment of silence, he said, "Okay. It's true. I'm scared."

Again I walked out into the streets. There were pink posters pasted onto the walls with long columns listing the names of people who had been executed for "crimes against the Reich." Often, there were three or four people with the same surname: whole families murdered for trying to help someone like me.

Marta's house was in a suburb high up on a hill and I got caught in two air raids before I reached it. Air raids were as dangerous as streetcars. The police and air raid wardens checked the papers of all strangers who entered the shelters but if you tried to stay in the street, which was strictly forbidden, you would almost surely be seen.

Both times, I managed to slip into a passageway where I passed the time trying to imagine what Marta was doing. It was not hard to guess. She would be painting, because that was her life. And she was probably still waiting on Vlada because that, too, was her life. Now, at noon, she was probably just putting aside her brushes and beginning to prepare Vlada's lunch. I should hurry up and get there before he returned home.

When Marta first saw me she shrank back, but then her whole face lit up with pleasure. She sat me down in her warm kitchen, and all of a sudden I felt so tired that I could not manage more than a few sentences. For Marta though, even those were enough.

"It's great you came here," she said. "Now you'll have nothing to worry about. Vlada will help you. Don't look so surprised! It's true. I know what you think of him. I have to admit I was starting to agree with you and I finally told him that if he didn't change, I was leaving him. Believe me, he took it to heart. You'll see for yourself. To make a long story short, Vlada started working for the Resistance! He helps hide fugitives; he works with the partisans! Can you believe it? At first he didn't want to talk about it but you know it's never too hard to get him talking about anything that makes him look good. And the point is that he's really doing something useful—look, he's coming! I'll go tell him you're here."

Marta disappeared down the hall and, when she came back, Vlada was behind her. He really had changed. He was no longer the charming playboy I remembered from before the war, good for nothing more than looks and pleasant chat. He was thinner, and his face was lined. Actually, he was better looking than before. But he did not meet my eyes. He just managed a crooked smile and stretched out his hand. It was cold as ice.

"Marta told me you escaped from the concentration camp," he said. "That's really something. I'd love to help you out, only there's a problem . . . "

"What?" said Marta. "Only last night you said. . . "

"Marta, something very unfortunate has happened. The man I was going to meet tonight will not come. Somehow the connection broke down. It's rotten luck, but we always knew that this kind of thing could happen."

"But surely you can do something. You keep telling me how everything's covered. You must have made plans for a situation like this."

"Of course, but it'll take time. Maybe a week. Ten days?"

"Fine," said Marta and turned to me. "You'll stay here until contact is restored. Vlada, we can hide her in the den by the attic. She'll be safe there and it's warm."

"Marta!" Sweat had broken out on Vlada's forehead. "Don't you know they shoot people for harboring illegals?"

"What's the matter with you? You're suddenly afraid to do something you've been doing all year? Or *said* you were doing— Vlada!"

Vlada collapsed into the nearest chair. Marta's face became so pale that her black eyes and hair looked as though they were painted onto the wall behind her. I got up and tiptoed out into the hall, then into the yard. Neither of them seemed to notice.

31

It was a long walk to Vinohrady, a neighborhood almost at the other end of the city, and my legs were beginning to give out by the time I got to the apartment where Otto and Milena lived. It was late afternoon when Otto opened the door. It took him a while to get his bearings, but Milena ran out past him and threw her arms around me.

"How great you got back! I was so afraid I'd never see you again! You'll stay with us. Don't worry, we'll hide you. You have to tell us everything, but first come and see my babies! Surprised? Then you'll lie down and rest. You look terrible. You'll have a nap and then I'll fix you something good to eat."

I allowed myself to be led into their bedroom and to be tucked in as though I were Milena's third child. Her mother covered me up, sat by me, and stroked my hair.

So I had, after all, found people and a place that had not changed, that had remained the same in the middle of all that destruction. Here I could catch my breath, if only for a day or two. Then I would set out for the woods and join the partisans . . . Otto and Milena would find some contact. Everything would be all right. No more roaming the streets . . . I did find someone . . . Who would have thought that of all people Milena would be the one not to be afraid? . . . Even though she has her mother to think of . . . and her children . . . those children!

I sat up in bed, my sleepiness gone. There was no way I could stay. Two small children! And that kind old lady! I must leave right away. How lucky that no one had seen me on the staircase!

I closed my eyes for one more minute, trying not to think. I had to go on, and in a few hours it would be night again. Then I got up and went into the kitchen where Otto and Milena and her mother were whispering together like a group of conspirators. Otto was even drafting some kind of blueprint; they probably wanted to wall up some corner of their tiny apartment for my hiding place.

First I had to give them a report. I made it short and, for the sake of Milena's mother, I skipped over the worst events. Then I asked about our other friends. How many were left? Only Zdena and Ruda. Zdena had married, but was living with her new husband in her parents' apartment just like before. Ruda one hardly ever saw. He was always out of town, Milena said, sometimes for months at a time. During the last year they had seen him only twice. Both times he showed up unexpectedly, tired and withdrawn. He sat for a while and then left.

Finally I told them I was leaving. They argued with me and tried to talk me into changing my mind, but soon realized that I would not stay. In the end, Milena fixed a large bag of food and other useful little things and extorted my promise to come back if I could not find another place to hide. But I knew this was a promise I would never keep.

Darkness had fallen over the city, and I was driven by only one thought: I had to find a place to sleep, I must not spend the night on the street. But there was no place to go. Then I remembered the Machs, a kind older couple who had known me since I was a child. They worked as superintendents in one of those new apartment houses in Strasnice where the apartments were like small cages. I knew I could not hide there, but I hoped they might help me find other shelter.

Mrs. Machova welcomed me with tears of joy, but then the shock overwhelmed her. She kept wandering around her apartment gathering things and then dropping them again in her confusion. She did not want to let me go but could not let me stay. At last she sat down at the kitchen table, covered her face with her hands, and broke down sobbing.

It was getting very late, and I got up to leave. At that moment, Mr. Mach, a shy, reticent man who up until this point had watched the two of us silently from his armchair, shouted, "Sit down you silly girl, damn it! We won't let you go. Now listen to me . . . " Then he explained that one of his tenants was away, and that his apartment would be empty until the next day. I could sleep there if I sneaked out very early the next morning.

The whole house was asleep when I ran up the darkened staircase, slipped through a strange doorway, and curled up on a strange couch in a strange apartment, as alert as a stray cat.

Long before another day dawned, I was outside again in the

cold, my footsteps the only sound in the streets. I had only one hope left: Zdena, the last of my prewar friends. It took me a long time to work up the courage to ring her doorbell. Her mother opened the door, chubby and smiling, holding in her arms a little boy just a few months old. She looked at me, aghast, and her face paled. She lifted the baby up and held him towards me like a cross against the Antichrist, and hissed, "For God's sake, go away! Can't you see? This child! For the sake of the child, go! Please! Go!"

I ran down the stairs. Damn! Damn it all! No more of this. No more pleading. No more begging for help. This is the end. I want to survive but at this price life is too expensive. If things continued this way, there would be no people left in my world. I would lose what even the camps and the war had not taken away from me.

I set out toward the city limits, to where the streets ended, and walked out into the fields. The smell of wet earth reminded me that only two days earlier we had been running, tripping on the frozen lumps of soil, telling ourselves, "On all fours, if we have to, but we'll make it home . . . " The sky was clear and high above and I could feel that winter was almost over. In two or three months spring would arrive. Then all the colors would change and maybe even the war would end. But for me it would be too late.

My escape into life had just not worked out. It had failed for reasons other than those that I had feared, but, in the end, that did not matter much because any kind of failure meant death. Still, it had been a magnificent attempt, even if it had failed, even though it would be harder to die now.

Just then I looked up and saw I was walking toward a small church. A refuge, at least for a short while! Surely there were no raids here. I went in and sank into a carved pew. There were very few people there, mostly women. I closed my eyes. Only a long time later did I feel something running down my cheeks. I felt no particular pain, no fear, no regret. I was just endlessly tired and distant from myself. I could not think or wish for anything and I just repeated to myself over and over again: life . . . life.

I was dimly aware of the priest delivering his sermon for a long while before I managed to listen. He was talking about the women who watched Christ suffer on the cross, who pitied him but did nothing to alleviate his pain. He then spoke of effective compassion, of helping one's fellow man. I wondered what would happen if I walked up to him after mass and said: Here's your opportunity to put your teachings to work. Help me. Let me sleep here in your little church for a few nights. As soon as I feel better, I'll be on my way. I thought about it from every possible angle but, in the end, rejected the idea. If my own friends had not been able to help me, what could I expect from a stranger? He might denounce me to the authorities right away. His sermon did not mean a thing. All those people who had chased me out into the street had voiced the same sentiments at one time or another and all had tried to persuade others of their duty to help friends in need.

I did not want to leave the church but, finally, there was no other way. A luminous dusk was descending over Prague. The day was beautiful, even now that it was dying. I wandered slowly through the city toward the Old Town. The river was not frozen and I thought that would be the best way to end it all. Of course the problem was I could swim like a fish. I would also have to take precautions against a last-minute rescue. Somewhere under a bridge I would pick up a few heavy rocks, put them in Milena's bag, and tie it to my neck with the belt of my coat.

Having worked out these technical details, I did not want to think about them anymore. But somehow I could think of nothing else, and it was not a pleasant stroll. My head was spinning. The skin of my whole body was smarting. I was feverish and the sores on my feet felt inflamed. The streets were full of people, and every once in a while I thought I caught a suspicious stare.

I got to a bridge and leaned over. Below me the river Vltava was flowing dark and cold, whispering to itself. The distance from the bridge to the water seemed enormous. So this was where my journey ended. This was the freedom no one could imagine—the freedom of a bird, the freedom of the wind, a freedom without people. A freedom without exit, lonely and as terrifying as the river below. I took off my gloves and put my hands on the cold stone of the bridge.

At that moment, two uniforms appeared on either side of me, pressed against me, and a harsh German dialect hit my ears. I stiffened with horror. So they had gotten me after all! At the very last moment. No! They would not get me alive! Jump! Right now! I tore myself away with all my remaining strength and one of the men laughed. Only then did I take a good look at them. They were not SS men, just ordinary soldiers. I stammered something incoherent and stumbled away. They did not try to hold me back. Even out of earshot, for a long time I could still hear their laughter, louder and louder. My head became an echo, a thundering bell. Spots of light flickered before my eyes, my heart refused to return to its usual place. I am really at the end of my rope, I thought. I cannot go on. So let the end come . . . any end. . . .

But it was too early. People were still strolling along the river, and it was not yet dark enough to return to the bridge. I dragged myself wherever my legs took me. The sidewalks seemed to heave with my every step. Streets, people, shadows, voices throbbing in my ears, streets, shadows. Only when I arrived in front of the apartment building where Ruda lived did I realize where I was.

I walked up and down in front of the house for a while. I had decided that I would not try to see anyone else. Ruda would not be home anyway. He might not even live here anymore. Some Germans might have requisitioned his apartment. It was dangerous and hopeless. Still, I wanted to do something: to walk, to think, to see, to postpone death for just a little bit longer. To have someone talk to me. To feel for one more moment that I still belonged to humanity.

I walked across the lobby and began to stagger up the stairs, clutching the railing. Ruda's name was still on the door. A thin thread of light showed through the peephole. To hell with caution, I thought. Everything is over anyway. I rang the bell. The door flew open as if someone had been waiting for me behind it, and Marta, pale, her black hair dishevelled, grabbed my hand and quickly pulled me into the apartment.

"Where have you been all this time? Where did you go? Why didn't you come here right after you left our house? I've been waiting for you and worrying like crazy!" Marta whispered and yelled and sobbed all at once. "Yesterday, right away—well, not right away, but as soon as I could—I ran here to see Ruda. I was sure this would be your next stop. Ruda's the only one of us worth anything. And you didn't know he's never in Prague these days, did you? It was a miracle that I found him here. He wasn't home for almost a year, and yesterday he was back for just one day. He promised to wait for you till morning, and when I came back today he gave me the keys and said you should stay here, that he'd take care of you. Since then I've been sitting here waiting. I could never forgive myself if anything had happened to you. Where were you?"

"I'll tell you some day," I said. "Right now I can't."

I was holding onto the door to keep myself from collapse. "What about Vlada?"

"You saw. He lied to me all these months. It was all make-believe. And yet I could have managed to forgive him if at least he had understood that you were giving him the chance to do something decent for once in his miserable life. But let's forget him for the moment. He's not the problem. You are. Stay here and wait. Be careful. The neighbors can hear every step. . . . "

Marta's face seemed to be getting bigger. Her voice was booming. The whole room was turning around me. I saw the apartment door close, heard the key turn in the lock and then drop with a clink through the mail slot—probably to fool the neighbors. By that time, I was already falling face down on the couch, feeling as though my body was breaking into a thousand pieces. The tension that had been holding me together suddenly relaxed. My stomach started to heave. Tremors ran down my spine and the walls around me threw back every heartbeat like an echo.

A few days went by, perhaps a week or two.

Gradually, the fever subsided. My head no longer ached and I could walk again. I found some food in the kitchen and I began to feel stronger. Then, one morning, someone dropped a letter through the mail slot. I brought it to the table by the sofa and let it sit there. I had to relish the feeling that someone knew I existed, that someone had thought of me and had taken the trouble to write me, had even brought the letter over by hand. When I opened it, I found a note printed in block letters:

COME AT SIX TO THE PARK BY THE CHURCH. I WILL BE WEARING A BROWN COAT, GREY HAT AND CAR-RYING A BLACK BRIEFCASE IN MY RIGHT HAND. SAY: I THINK WE HAVE MET SOMEWHERE BEFORE.

I spent the whole afternoon getting ready for my first walk. I was still weak with fever, but I had had some sleep and rest and the prospect of going out to meet someone made me feel alive.

The evening was wet and gloomy, and patches of snow were melting in the drizzle. I saw him from a distance, standing at the corner of the park: a thin man in a worn overcoat, briefcase in hand. I walked slowly toward him, hesitant. He looked me over carefully and then smiled.

"You need not say anything," he said. "Ruda sent me. Stop being afraid. We'll help you. Everything will be all right."

The whisper of the rain stopped and it began to snow. In the curve of the park path, behind a commotion of snowflakes, I could see the figure of a man. He walked like a machine, his steps sharp on the ground. I could tell it was an SS man even before I could make out the outline of his uniform. I gripped my companion's arm. The SS man came closer, jerked his head in our direction, returned it with another jerk, and passed by. I looked up at the man beside me and felt the snowflakes melt on my face. He smiled again and squeezed my hand.

We walked out of the park and into the streets. People passed by, snuggling into their coats, hurrying home to warm stoves and to doors they would shut behind them. We turned the corner onto a sharply sloped street that I had never walked before. In the dark and through all the snow, I could not see where it ended. We walked fast, in silence.

The war ended the way a passage through a tunnel ends. From far away you could see the light ahead, a gleam that kept growing, and its brilliance seemed ever more dazzling to you huddled there in the dark the longer it took to reach it. But when at last the train burst out into the glorious sunshine, all you saw was a wasteland full of weeds and stones, and a heap of garbage.

The last weeks of my underground existence seemed endless. I was so lonely that I spent most of my time listening to the radio, just to hear a human voice. But, since the broadcasts were made up of lies about the victorious advance of the German armies and other vicious Nazi propaganda, what those voices were saying was far from human. My only solace were the fairy tales broadcast for children. I used to fall asleep wishing that the next day the broadcast would be one long fairy tale and that the voices on the radio would speak only in the language of children, elves, and enchanted animals.

One evening, my friends from the Resistance brought in a wounded Russian partisan debilitated by fever. They put him down on the bed and left me alone with him and the icon which he took from his knapsack and hung on the wall. I nursed him for two days, shared my few stale crackers with him, and prayed that he would not die. When they took him away on the third night, I felt even lonelier than before.

Once or twice I was transferred to another hiding place because staying too long in the same spot meant almost certain discovery. In early April, I moved into my last secret residence, an empty apartment in the posh suburb of Dejvice. The weather was unusually warm; spring was surging into the city before its time. The sunshine lit up the pale, impassive face of Prague and, almost overnight, restored its natural splendor.

I could no longer remain behind locked doors and closed windows. Every day I ventured out and strolled for hours under the greening trees, through streets which seemed to stir with my own impatience and craving for a return to life. This, of course, was very foolish. Had I been caught by the Gestapo and tortured, I might have jeopardized the lives of all the people who had helped me and endangered Ruda's whole group of partisans.

At night I listened to the BBC, which transmitted news and information in Czech as well as coded messages for the Resistance groups. The penalty for owning a short-wave radio set was death. Hundreds of people had been shot on the spot for this crime, but thousands more kept listening to these broadcasts from London and then spreading the news.

One night at the beginning of May I heard the code name of Ruda's group on the BBC broadcast and guessed that the few words which followed were a signal for the final decisive action. The next night Ruda himself arrived, covered up to his ears in mud, and pulled out the weapons that lay concealed behind a false partition in a huge closet.

"Next time I come back," he said, "the war will be over."

Then, on the fifth day of May, the regular broadcast on Radio Prague was suddenly interrupted by the crackling sound of gunshots and a new voice, a very human voice, shouted, "Come help us everyone! We are fighting the Germans!" and called upon the whole population of Prague to rise up and liberate the city. I rushed to the window and saw men, some of them with rifle in hand, already running down the street.

People started digging in their basements, under the compost heaps of their gardens, in the middle of flower beds. They slashed mattresses and their grandmothers' sofas; they ripped out floorboards. Secret vaults in factories and warehouses, even coffins in some cemeteries were opened, and the weapons that had been hidden there for years were taken out and hurriedly distributed. Barricades sprang up in the streets with miraculous speed. The freedom fighters pinned on tricolors—the time-honored badges of liberty—and the final act of the war, the first and last battle for Prague, began.

I ran out of the house toward a major avenue and joined a group of young people on a barricade, but it soon became clear that I was not likely to distinguish myself in armed combat. It did not matter. I felt there had been too much death and killing in my life already, so I turned to the only place where I could be of some use, to the makeshift Red Cross center that had been set up in a basement cinema, where the Resistance headquarters for the suburb of Dejvice was also situated. There I ran into a set of people very different from the brave, determined crowd in the street.

The headquarters was staffed mostly by affluent-looking gentlemen, former officers of the Czechoslovak Army which had been disbanded in 1939. Now, at the last minute, they seemed eager to establish for themselves a record of resistance against the Germans. It was obvious that they knew very little about the strategy of street fighting. They sat for hours around a table, comfortably discussing the theory and tactics of warfare while their commanding officer, a colonel who had only the vaguest conception of the situation outside, kept issuing pointless orders to the eighteen-year-olds whose fathers and brothers had been murdered by the Germans and who now fought and died on the barricades.

In the first-aid center, nearly all the volunteer nurses were well-dressed suburban housewives, who devoted the greater part of their energy to effusive displays of patriotism and to flirtations with the doctors and officers, leaving all the hard work to the few professional Red Cross nurses.

There was one important service the underground center provided: it was a depository and distribution post for weapons, ammunition, medical supplies, and provisions that were smuggled in from outside. Often an old, half-starved pensioner would sneak through the streets under fire to bring us a loaf of bread saved from his meager ration, a crumpled packet of cigarettes, a bottle of prewar rum. Later, many of these precious gifts disappeared into the large shopping bags that our volunteer nurses had providently brought along.

Our small supply of weapons was nearly gone when word came from a Resistance group operating near the railway station that we could have more if two volunteers, possibly Red Cross nurses, would come and pick them up. There had been a large cache of weapons hidden under the railway station ever since the Nazis had occupied Czechoslovakia. Now the railway men, many of whom were active members of the Resistance, were managing to smuggle the guns out of the station right under the noses of the Germans.

I offered to go and someone handed me a nurse's cap and pinned a band with a red cross around my sleeve.

"We need another person," said the Colonel.

After a few moments of embarrassed silence, an elderly woman in a nurse's uniform stepped forward. "I'm coming," she said.

The fighting in the streets was heavy. We had to run from doorway to doorway and sprint across several intersections. The old woman was breathless but did not slow down.

As we approached the station, we saw the station master chatting with two heavily-armed German soldiers who were standing guard. On the pavement in front of them stood a huge oval laundry basket. It had a handle on each end and was covered with a white sheet on which someone had painted a large, crooked red cross. We each grasped a handle, lifted the basket and walked away. As soon as we were out of sight, though, we stopped in a doorway and looked under the sheet. The weapons on the bottom of the basket were covered with a layer of small boxes, packs of cotton wool, and rolls of bandages.

The way back proved rather difficult. We could not run with the heavy basket between us and had to stay close to the sides of buildings from which bullets ricocheted in short spurts like hail. We had turned the last corner back to headquarters when we almost bumped into a very young German soldier with an automatic rifle. We stopped dead and the nurse, startled, dropped her handle. The basket tilted, hit the ground, and something inside made a sharp clink. The soldier jumped back, crouched behind his rifle and, pointing it first at her, then at me, started shouting. I looked at my partner. Her face under the white cap was as gray as her hair. She's going to faint, I thought. But at that moment she began to speak in a soothing hospital voice.

"We're just bringing back some medical supplies for the wounded," she said in good German. "Would you like to have a roll of gauze for yourself? It might come in handy, you know."

She uncovered the basket and held out one of the packages. The young boy in the soldier's uniform took it from her obediently, staring, with his mouth slightly open. We grabbed our handles and walked as fast as we could the few hundred yards that remained between us and the shelter.

I shall always remember that woman with love. If courage is the capacity to conquer one's fear, she was the most courageous person I have ever met.

Among the volunteers who had come to pluck a bit of cheap glory for themselves in the Red Cross center was a former schoolmate of mine, well-groomed and elegant. You could see that she had taken good care of herself during the war and had avoided any trouble; even now, she was careful to remain in the background. But, as the situation in the streets worsened, our first-aid station filled up, and we all had our hands full. It was then that she saw me giving a glass of water to a dying German soldier and said, "If I didn't know you had been in a concentration camp, I'd make sure you paid for this. Didn't you hear what the doctor said? Take care of the Czechs and let the Germans go to hell!"

That was my first frightening glimpse of the devastation, the deep corrosion that the war had inflicted upon us. It had divided people like the slash of a knife, and that wound would take a long time to heal.

Although their war was lost and the Russian armies were hard on their heels, the German troops, the Gestapo, and the SS men put up a ferocious fight in Prague. The SS, especially, were determined to make the most of their last days in power. Even while fleeing the city, they took the time to jump out of their cars in the relatively quiet suburbs, break into basements where women, children, and old people were hiding, and shoot them all. More SS troops in heavy armor descended daily on the city. The shortage of guns and ammunition became critical.

On the fifth day of the uprising, when the fighting on our side was no more than a desperate effort to gain time, a column of tanks marked with red stars suddenly rolled into the torn-up streets. Out jumped weather-beaten, fair-haired men with machine guns. It took them but a few hours to put the stubborn Germans to flight.

People streamed into the streets to cheer, to welcome, to embrace their liberators, asking them into their homes, offering them every good thing they had. Pretty girls covered the tanks with flowers and climbed onto the armored trucks. The Russians laughed good-naturedly and took out their accordions. The world was full of fragrance and music and joy.

When the Germans finally withdrew, I could go outside for the first time in years without fear. The day before, a bullet had grazed my leg, and I could not walk without difficulty. Slowly I limped out of the house down along a narrow footpath we called the "mouse hole" that had been worn down through the lilac bushes to the riverbank. The air was quiet, sweet with the scent of lilac, and only now and then did a shot ring out as people combing parks and attics discovered the last Germans in hiding.

I walked out onto Klarov, into the open space before the bridge. There was not a living soul anywhere, only Prague spread out above and around me in an embrace. It was that moment just before sunset, when outlines briefly become sharp and clear and colors more brilliant, reminding us that the night is short, that darkness comes and then goes again. I walked a few steps farther and saw, down by the bridge, a man in the black uniform of the SS, lying in a puddle of black blood. Prague glowed and arched above that black puddle and the black, now harmless, thing lying in it and I said to myself, "Now, at this moment and on this spot, the war is over, because he is dead and I am alive."

And so ended that horrible long war that refuses to be forgotten. Life went on. It went on despite both the dead and the living, because this was a war that no one had quite survived. Something very important and precious had been killed by it or, perhaps, it had just died of horror, of starvation, or simply of disgust—who knows? We tried to bury it quickly, the earth settled over it, and we turned our backs on it impatiently. After all, our real life was now beginning and what to make of it was up to us.

People came crawling out of their hide-outs. They came back from the forests, from the prisons, and from the concentration camps, and all they could think was, "It's over; it's all over." I remember a boy whose wooden clogs had to be surgically removed from his feet because his soles had grown into them. I remember Eliska who had passed through Auschwitz twice, twice escaped the gas chambers, and then walked all the way back to Prague. There she sat down before the statue of St. Wenceslas, kissed the ground, and fainted. The ambulance took her to a hospital, where she died within a week because she had no lungs left. And Mr. Lustig who spent the entire war hidden in a closet and almost lost his eyesight. But he was lucky; he survived. Then, during the uprising, he walked out into the daylight for the first time and, after barely a few steps, he was shot right through the head.

Some people came back silent, and some talked incessantly as though talking about a thing would make it vanish. Actually, just the opposite is true: once things and thoughts are expressed and described they acquire a new reality, as though by giving them words we give them part of ourselves. After that, they will not allow us to leave them behind.

While some voices spoke of death and flames, of blood and gallows, in the background, a chorus of thousands repeated tirelessly, "You know, we also suffered . . . Nothing but skimmed milk . . . No butter on our bread. . . . "

Sometimes a bedraggled and barefoot concentration camp survivor plucked up his courage and knocked on the door of prewar friends to ask, "Excuse me, do you by any chance still have some of the stuff we left with you for safekeeping?" And the friends would say, "You must be mistaken, you didn't leave anything with us, but come in anyway!" And they would seat him in their parlor where his carpet lay on the floor and pour herb tea into antique cups that had belonged to his grandmother. The survivor would thank them, sip his tea, and look at the walls where his paintings hung. He would say to himself, "What does it matter? As long as we're alive? What does it matter?"

At other times, it would not turn out so nicely. The prewar friends would not make tea, would not suggest any mistake. They would just laugh and say in astonishment, "Come on now, do you really believe we would store your stuff all through the war, exposing ourselves to all that risk just to give it back to you now?" And the survivor would laugh too, amazed at his own stupidity, would apologize politely and leave. Once downstairs he would laugh again, happily, because it was spring and the sun was shining down on him.

It would also happen that a survivor might need a lawyer to retrieve lost documents and he would remember the name of one who had once represented large Jewish companies. He would go to see him and sit in an empire chair in a corner of an elegant waiting room, enjoying all that good taste and luxury, watching pretty secretaries rushing about. Until one of the pretty girls forgot to close a door behind her, and the lawyer's sonorous voice would boom through the crack, "You would have thought we'd be rid of them finally, but no, they're impossible to kill off—not even Hitler could manage it. Every day there're more of them crawling back, like rats . . . " And the survivor would quietly get up from his chair and slip out of the waiting room, this time not laughing. On his way down the stairs his eyes would mist over as if with the smoke of the furnaces at Auschwitz.

Friends from the country would send an invitation: Come see us! We want to feed you. We have plenty of everything! The survivor would arrive at the village, unable to believe his eyes. The farmhouse would be twice its prewar size. A refrigerator would be standing in the kitchen, a washing machine in the hall. There would be Oriental carpets on the floor and original paintings on the walls. The sausage would be served on silver platters and the beer in cut glass. The old farmer would stroke his whiskers and worry, "No sense denying it—we did very well during the war. People had to eat, you know, and with a little thinking . . . But now things are different . . . Just as long as the Communists don't take over . . . "

It took me some time to muster up the courage for a trip to the village of Hut where we used to spend our vacations. Our country house there was as much of a home to me as our apartment in Prague had been, maybe even more so for all the happy memories it held. To return there all alone, the only one of my family who was left, was hard. On the way out the train seemed to be moving too fast, the air was hot and stifling, my head throbbed, and my stomach ached. In Beroun, where I had to change trains, I was seized with such anxiety that I almost returned to Prague. At last I reached Hut and made my way haltingly from the station to the village, glimpsing from far away those windows where I used to see my mother looking out, alive and happy.

The trees in our orchard were past their bloom and no one seemed to be about. The door of our house was locked. I rang the bell and, after a while, a fat unshaven man opened the door, stared at me for a moment, and then yelled, "So you've come back! Oh no! That's all we needed!"

I turned around and walked into the woods. I spent the three hours until the next train back to Prague strolling on the mossy ground under the fir trees, listening to the birds.

Perhaps everything would have turned out differently if the war had ended in autumn instead of in spring. The rain and mud would have forced people to keep their eyes on the ground. But the spring of 1945 was so beautiful, Prague in the splendor of her gardens was so dazzling, that we became blind to the ominous shadows, to the warning signs of an uneasy future.

I spent whole days wandering through Prague, stumbling over broken cobblestones. Sometimes I ran into people who turned their backs on me but others took me home with them, fed me, and asked concerned, thoughtful questions. Once I met my mother's dressmaker, who burst into tears, took me by the hand, and led me to her workroom. There she made a dress for me on the spot from all kinds of remnants she had saved during the war and, through it all, she never stopped crying.

Every day I listened to the radio, anxious to hear news of liberated prisoners. Occasionally there would be a familiar name. Then, once, the voice on the air said, "Brother Ervin Bloch has arrived in Prague and is organizing the return of other prisoners . . . "

Ervin Bloch was my father's name. His emaciated white face flashed before my eyes as I had seen him last, after we got off the train at the railway station in Auschwitz, among a group of people destined to die. His eyes said: Good-bye, take care of your mother. But my mother had been torn away from me a few minutes later and, when I ran after her, a soldier with a submachine gun grabbed my shoulder and knocked me to the ground. By that time the handsome Dr. Mengele had already beckoned, and my mother was swallowed by the thousand-headed serpent which was disappearing into a windowless building in the distance. I rose from the dirt, stunned. I glimpsed only my mother's arms reaching out toward me as if she were drowning. That soldier with the submachine gun was still standing there and I shouted at him, "What's going to happen to them? What are you going to do with them?" But he only grinned derisively. "Shut up! Nothing's happening. You'll see them again in a few hours." Then a girl in a striped shift who had a shaven head brushed against me and whispered, "Don't believe him. You'll never see them again. They burn them all." At that moment, the whole world exploded in fire and smoke and that fire burned my brain to ashes so that only one cell was left. That one cell flickered on and off like a signal light for weeks on end and, each time it lit up, it shone on my mother and father as they fell with outstretched arms into the flames.

Now my father was returning home! Was it possible that he was still alive? That by some miracle he had been saved at the last minute? I jumped up from my chair and, in an instant, was in the street, limping furiously downhill toward the radio station. Public transportation had not yet been restored in the shattered city, and I had quite a long way to go.

As far as two blocks away I saw that the street was packed with people trying to get inside the radio station, into the only center of information about those who were returning and those who had disappeared. I looked at that impenetrable wall of backs with despair; somehow, I had to get inside. Then suddenly, a couple of people looked at me and of their own accord stepped aside. One head after another started to turn and, slowly, a path opened up before me. Someone even gave me a little shove, so that I flew up to the front of the crowd like a bullet. Even the man standing watch at the door took just one look at me and opened it.

A while later I stood in a tiny office with the man charged with broadcasts for the liberated prisoners. He was terribly thin, his head was a skull covered with skin, and his eyes were half-closed with fatigue. He thought for a moment and said, "I don't have a minute free in the whole broadcast. I get calls from hundreds of people begging me to include the briefest message. It's impossible; there's simply no time. But sit down. Wait. Maybe I'll manage to squeeze in a few words here or there."

I sat at the radio station hour after hour. Once in a while the voice on the monitor repeated my father's name and asked him to call the station where his daughter was waiting for him. But no one called. The skinny man turned to me every so often and finally said, "Listen, there's no reason to lose hope yet. I do a newscast late at night that all the prisoners listen to. I'll mention your father's name again and if he's alive, I'm sure he'll answer. Go home. I'll call if I learn anything."

I returned to the empty apartment in Dejvice where I still spent my nights and huddled in a chair by the radio listening to that voice summoning a father who had not been alive for a long time, who had only a name in common with the stranger who had returned home. But, two days later, the telephone rang.

"Unfortunately, we could not find your father," the kind voice said, "but today we got a letter from a Rudolf Margolius. He escaped from Dachau and the Americans have named him commander of a camp for former prisoners in Garmisch-Partenkirchen, in charge of repatriation. He heard my newscast and sent me a report about the situation in the camp. But mainly he asked about you. Your name is Heda right? Listen again tonight, and I'll answer him."

I sat there clutching the receiver, unable to utter a word. The kind man laughed a little and said, "Good luck."

For months I had tried, not very successfully, to think of Rudolf as little as possible, to hope as little as possible, knowing how slim the chance was that both of us had survived and afraid that the disappointment of that hope would be too hard to bear.

And yet Rudolf was alive! Rudolf, the best man in the world, my man, the man with whom I would spend the rest of my life.

I put down the receiver and, as always when my emotions overwhelmed me, went for a walk. I turned into a park and started ravaging a flower bed. Two children, a small boy and an older girl, stood on the path and watched me with disapproval.

"You shouldn't pick the tulips," said the little boy. "It's not allowed."

"Oh, yes, I'm allowed," I said. "At least today I am. I'm celebrating."

"What are you celebrating?" asked the girl. "The end of the war?"

I thought for a moment.

"No," I said. "The beginning of peace."

That evening I sat again by the radio thinking that at the very same moment, somewhere in a camp high up in the mountains, Rudolf was sitting and listening too, hearing the same voice, the same words.

The voice said, "We thank Rudolf Margolius for his report and are pleased to tell him that . . . "

Only much later did I learn that Rudolf had only heard the first three words of that sentence when the power failed in Garmisch, silencing all radios and leaving his question without an answer.

From that night on, the Czechs in his camp whiled away their hours of boredom in betting whether or not I was the Heda of the broadcast. The repatriation from Garmisch was completed toward the middle of June, and Rudolf only returned to Prague with the very last group of freed prisoners. When they reached the railway station, no one got off the train. They stood at the windows and doors watching Rudolf dial the number of the radio station from a telephone booth on the platform. When he hung up, they called out, "Was it Heda?"

Rudolf nodded, and only then did they jump off the cars and hurry home.

Two months after liberation, people had stopped cheering and embracing. They were not giving away food and clothing anymore, but selling it on the black market. Those who had compromised their integrity during the Occupation now began to calculate and plan, to watch and spy on each other, to cover their tracks, eager to secure the property they had acquired through collaboration with the Germans, by cowardice or denunciation, or by looting the homes of deported Jews. Their sense of guilt and fear of retribution soon bred hate and suspicion directed mainly at the real victims of the Occupation: the active and passive resisters, the partisans, the Jews, and political prisoners; the honest people who had stood their ground and had not betrayed their principles even at the cost of persecution. The innocent became a living reproach and a potential threat to the guilty.

Now these survivors, dead-tired from standing in endless lines for documents, ration cards, and food, disgusted by the petty skirmishes with bureaucrats and profiteers, began to worry seriously about the future of the country. It was becoming evident to many that while evil grows all by itself, good can be achieved only through hard struggle and maintained only through tireless effort, that we had to set out clear, boldly-conceived goals for ourselves and join forces to attain them. The problem was that everyone envisioned these goals differently.

52

For all those whom the war had displaced, the biggest worry was housing. Partisans who throughout the war had lived in the woods, widows of the executed who for years had slept on the floor of some basement, and ailing survivors of the concentration camps all spent day after day waiting in lines at the Housing Authority while butchers and grocers and other wartime profiteers walked in by the back door and were seen first. Most of them already had good apartments, but now that they had become rich they wanted better ones. There were a number of empty apartments in Prague, abandoned by the Germans, beautifully decorated with furniture that had once belonged to Jews, so how about it? Hadn't the butchers and grocers supplied the bureaucrats at City Hall with meat and flour throughout the war? Weren't they now entitled to a little recognition for their efforts?

Meanwhile, in the waiting room, a clerk would yell at the women who stood there weeping: "What do you want me to do? So many of you came back—how do you think we can find housing for you all? You expect miracles?" And people would walk out, humiliated, their fists clenched in rage.

I have often thought that many of our people turned to Communism not so much in revolt against the existing political system, but out of sheer despair over human nature which showed itself at its very worst after the war. Since it is impossible for men to give up on mankind, they blame the social order in which they live; they condemn the human condition.

In the end, I wound up with an apartment sooner then Mr. Boucek, the owner of a poultry store whom I would often see conferring with the clerks at the Housing Authority. Of course, he was after something luxurious, while all I wanted was a roof over my head.

One evening, just before the building closed, I marched into the office of the chairman of the Housing Authority with a shopping bag containing all my possessions, mostly gifts from friends, and declared that I would sleep right there in the office for as long as I remained homeless because I had no other place to go. That was true. I had spent the last few nights in various improvised shelters for displaced persons. Before that, I had used up the store of my acquaintances who were willing to give me a place to stay; I had decided that I would not take advantage of their patience any longer. Besides, I thought it was about time I slept in my own bed after all these years.

The chairman of the Housing Authority began to fume, but I paid no attention to him. Slowly, I unpacked my bag. I took out a cake of soap, then a toothbrush, then a glass. Next to it I laid out a white napkin, and on it a slice of bread, a piece of cheese, and a bottle of milk. I draped a towel and my nightgown over an office chair. Then I sat down in the chairman's chair, poured myself a glass of milk, and bit into the bread. The chairman was still ranting. I finished eating and, very slowly, started taking off my shoes. Then I opened the first button of my blouse, silently praying for something, anything, to happen. I undid the second button. The chairman's face reddened. He wiped the sweat off his neck and shot out of the office.

I put my feet up on another chair, lit a cigarette—another precious gift—and waited. Some time later, there was a knock on the door and, after my pleasant invitation to enter, the door opened a crack and the chairman's bald pate appeared. Reassured that my preparations for the night had not proceeded any further, he let out a sigh of relief, beckoned to someone behind him, and came in. He was followed by his underling, a clerk who had previously told me many times that he understood my situation and would be only too happy to help me, but that he could not give me an apartment because he did not have one. Now he held a piece of paper toward me and said, "If we give you this deed right now so that you can move in tomorrow, will you please go away?"

I signed the deed, finished my glass of milk, and asked if they wished to share with me what remained in the bottle. They refused politely, and the chairman folded up my things with his own hands and put them back in my shopping bag. I took the bag and the deed and went to have a look at the house in which I would live. I seem to remember that the Housing Authority was eventually shut down because of corruption, but I am not certain.

54

The apartment was so tiny that two years later, when I was expecting a baby, Rudolf had to do all the cooking, because I could not fit between the stove and the wall. But there were lots of bookshelves and the sun shone in all day long. Friends came to visit, bringing mugs and dishes and blankets and pillows and, by the end of the summer, we were already calling it home.

Those shelves filled up quickly with books about politics and economics, old and torn, that Rudolf studied endlessly, and with a lot of new pamphlets printed on cheap paper, which I devoured. They offered such clear and simple answers to the most complicated questions that I kept feeling there had to be a mistake somewhere.

All injustice, discrimination, misery, and war, I read, stem from the fact that the handful of people who wield power are unwilling to relinquish their acquisitive urge, their exploitation of the working class, and their lust for world domination. As soon as the working people—the creators of all value—understand what must be done, they will overthrow the exploiters and their henchmen, will reeducate them as well as themselves, and the kingdom of heaven will come to earth. The real enemies of man are those who take profit from the sweat and callouses of others. If we divide the riches of the world equally, and apply ourselves to the work at hand, each according to his ability, society will see to it that no one wants for anything.

We shall no longer fight one another for an ever-larger slice of the economic pie. We shall pool our efforts and build happiness and prosperity for all. The soil belongs to the people who till it, the factories to those who work in them. At first, of course, it will be necessary to take a firm stand against the rich; those in power will not voluntarily give up their privileges. No capitalist will give up his position without a fight. But once the new order is established, even the capitalist will understand that progress toward a better society cannot be stopped. Eventually, unwilling to be left behind, he too will join our effort. We shall all be brothers, regardless of language or race. Only capitalism breeds racism; in a socialist society, all people are equal. Democracy, a progressive idea when first conceived, has degenerated and played out its role in history; today, it affords capitalists the opportunity to exploit and the unemployed the opportunity to beg. The capitalist economy inevitably leads to depression, and depression to fascism and war. The bourgeoisie has brought the world to the brink of destruction. Do you want to see another war in a decade or two? The last of all wars, a nuclear catastrophe? Isn't it time to change the world?

Let us go out and convince others, explain our ideas and goals. We do not wish to force people to change: people have to see the light by themselves and learn from their own experience. We can only help them toward an understanding by disseminating our ideas, our own—the only scientific truth.

Why do wars happen? See pages 45 through 47! What causes economic depressions? See page 66! Does God exist? What is truth? Marxism provides the answers to all these questions and offers solutions to problems which have plagued mankind since the dawn of history. The great change we are calling for is within our reach: people can change the conditions under which they live and through this change, man himself will eventually be transformed.

Friends—all of them young—came to visit Rudolf and me in our small apartment. They sat on the floor because there was no other place to sit and debated till morning. There was hardly an opinion that was not defended by someone, hardly an idea that went unproposed. Usually, I sat in a corner and just listened. I knew nothing about politics and less than nothing about economics. But I began to understand that life had become politics and politics had become life. It would not do anymore to say, "I don't care. I just want to be left in peace and quiet."

Whenever anyone defended the principles of democracy that I had been raised to believe, something inside me cried out, Yes, that's the way it is! But then I became uncertain when I heard the objections. The principles on which the prewar Czechoslovak Republic had been founded, the humanistic, democratic ideals of Thomas G. Masaryk, were an unrealistic illusion. Our democracy had allowed the growth of the fascist and Nazi parties which had in the end destroyed it. Worst of all, it had failed to defend the country against Hitler. After Munich, where our treacherous allies had forsaken us, our democratic government had surrendered to the Germans without a struggle.

Did we want to repeat the same mistakes and live out a new version of Munich? Who had sold us out to Hitler? Our allies the Western capitalists. Who had offered us help when every other country had abandoned us? The Soviet Union. Who had liberated Prague while the American army stood watching from Pilsen, some undefended fifty miles away? The Soviet Union.

Once two friends that Rudolf had known since childhood met in our home. Zdenek's father, a factory worker who had been unemployed for years before the war, had joined the Resistance soon after the Occupation. The Germans had arrested, then executed him. Zdenek himself had spent all the years of the war with the partisans. He limped awkwardly on feet that had been frostbitten during the war, but when he entered a room he brought with him that familiar self-assurance and strength of people for whom hardship is a challenge, an opportunity to measure oneself, to see how far one can stretch the limit of one's will, personality, humanity. Zdenek had been accepted into the Communist Party somewhere in the forest, in a tent, by candlelight, with a submachine gun in his hands.

The other friend was Franta, one of the people who had refused to help me during those first days after my escape from the camp. He had survived the entire war living quietly, inconspicuously, in Prague. He had done nothing dishonorable. He had not collaborated with the Nazis nor had he denounced anyone. But he had not taken any risks either. Although he had completed his military service before the war as an officer in the Czechoslovak army, it had never entered his mind that he should join the Resistance. He lived out the war like a hibernating animal. He had gained nothing, but he had also lost very little.

Later on, I would often remember the conversation between these two men. Every argument Franta made for democracy sounded right and reasonable to me. But every argument Zdenek made for communism was supported by the force of his personality and his experiences. Anything he said sounded strong and convincing simply because it was he who said it. As I listened to him, I felt almost ashamed to be agreeing with his opponent, Franta, who was so rational and prudent and who never forgot which side his bread was buttered on. It seemed unthinkable to choose Franta's side in this confrontation between caution and courage. That evening, as usual, the debate ended in total disagreement. Only the discord between these two men was unusually sharp. Theirs was not only a clash of views but of two worlds, two contradictory sets of concepts, feelings, and visions.

Much later, during the tormented haze of the fifties, when I would try, foolishly, to pinpoint the moment when our good will and enthusiasm betrayed us, when we took our first step toward desolation and destruction, I would think of that evening. Rudolf listened carefully to the two men and entered into the debate only occasionally. But I could see that his heart was completely with Zdenek, surely in part because he had never forgiven Franta for his cowardly behavior toward me. If his reason still posed objections to Zdenek's arguments, Rudolf had obviously decided to ignore them. The Communists at that time kept stressing the scientific basis of their ideology, but I know that the road that led many people into their ranks in Czechoslovakia was paved with good and strong emotions.

Rudolf was a very quiet, serious man, utterly unselfish. The experience of the concentration camps and the Occupation had affected him more deeply than anyone else I knew. He never overcame the humiliation that he—a young, healthy man, an officer in the Czechoslovak army—had allowed himself to be thrown into a camp without resisting and had looked on like a helpless cripple while people were murdered all around him. He had often risked his life to help his fellow inmates—they would come tell me about it themselves—but the memory of his helplessness and a sense of guilt never stopped torturing him. Now he believed more than ever before that every individual should aim to contribute to the common good, but he doubted that this could be achieved by means that had failed so miserably before.

About a week after Zdenek and Franta had spent the evening with us, Rudolf took me to see some of his friends, prewar Communist intellectuals who had lived in the Soviet Union during the war. They were a middle-aged couple who had a nice house, furnished in tasteful, totally unproletarian style. They were well-educated, very kind, and I felt quite at home with them. The wife discussed housekeeping with me and suggested ways to prepare the canned pork that came to us from the United Nations relief fund so that it would taste Czech. We asked them to tell us about their life in the Soviet Union. With tears in their eyes, they described the self-sacrifice and the patriotism of even the simplest Russians, their endurance and steadfast belief in eventual victory over the Nazis. They spoke about the profound feeling of brotherhood that reigned within the Soviet Union, the equality of the various nationalities and races, the fervor with which people performed even the hardest labor and the most dangerous tasks for their country; they described the solicitude of the Party and of the Soviet government, the friendly acceptance that they and other refugees had enjoyed. We left deeply impressed.

Two days later, Rudolf brought home applications for membership in the Communist Party.

Ten years later, the old lady who had been our hostess confessed that nearly everything she and her husband told us during our visit had been untrue. They had suffered hard times in Russia. People had been afraid to talk to them. Black marketeering, collaboration, anti-Semitism were rampant. Many people died unnecessary deaths. But since they did not dare, for the most part, to guess at the cause of their suffering, they died blessing the Party and Stalin with their last breath.

Our conditioning for the revolution had begun in the concentration camps. Perhaps we had been most impressed by the example of our fellow prisoners, Communists who often behaved like beings of a higher order. Their idealism and Party discipline gave them a strength and an endurance that the rest of us could not match. They were like well-trained soldiers in a crowd of children.

But there were other things too. All survivors remember to this day the stubborn determination which dominated that time, the total concentration on a single goal, the end of the war. Life was not life in any proper sense; it was only a thrust in that one direction. All our thinking and doing justified itself by the prospect of the future. The present only existed to be overcome, somehow, anyhow.

When the war finally ended, our joy soon changed into a sense of anticlimax and a yearning to fill the void that this intensity of expectation and exertion of will had left behind. A strong sense of solidarity had evolved in the concentration camps, the idea that one individual's fate was in every way tied to the fate of the group, whether that meant the group of one's fellow prisoners, the whole nation, or even all of humanity. For many people, the desire for material goods largely disappeared. As much as we longed for the comforts of life, for good food, clothing, and homes, it was clear to us that these things were secondary, and that our happiness and the meaning of our lives lay elsewhere. I remember how some of our fellow citizens for whom the war years had been a time of acquisition and hoarding, stared when we did not try to retrieve stolen property, to apply for restitution, to seek inheritances from relatives. This was true not only of Rudolf and myself but of any number of people who had come to identify their own well-being with the common good and who, rather logically, ended up in the most ideologically alluring political party—that of the Communists.

The years of imprisonment had yet another paradoxical effect. Although we continually hoped for freedom, our concept of freedom had changed. Shut up behind barbed wire, robbed of all rights including the right to live, we had stopped regarding freedom as something natural and self-evident. Gradually, the idea of freedom as birthright became blurred. By the end of their time in the camps, many prisoners came to accept the view that freedom is something that has to be earned and fought for, a privilege that is awarded, like a medal. It is hardly possible for people to live for so many years as slaves in everyday contact with fascists and fascism without becoming somewhat twisted, without contracting a trace of that dry rot unwittingly and unwillingly. Usually, the reasoning went something like this: if, for the purpose of building a new society, it is necessary to give up my freedom for a time, to subsume something I cherish to a cause in which I strongly believe, that is a sacrifice I am willing to make. In any case, we are a lost generation. We all might have died uselessly in the camps. Since we did survive, we want to dedicate what is left of our lives to the future.

This streak of martyrdom was stronger than was generally understood. People felt chosen by destiny to sacrifice themselves, a feeling that was reinforced by a strong sense of guilt that characterized many who had survived the camps. Why was I alive and not my father, my mother, my friend? I owed them something. They had died in place of me. For their sake I had to build a world in which this could never happen again.

This was where the misconception lay: in the idea that communism was the one system under which it could never happen again. Of course we knew about the communism of the thirties in the Soviet Union, but that was an era of cruelty that had ended long ago, the kind of crisis out of which all great change is born. Who, today, would condemn democracy for the Terror of the Jacobins after the French Revolution?

The most eagerly embraced belief of the time was that no national or racial oppression could exist under communism. Factual evidence to the contrary was hard to come by, and more persuasive than any piece of propaganda were the fairy tales of life in the Soviet Union spread by Czech Communists such as our middle-aged friends who had spent the war years there.

Many of those people lied with an eye to being rewarded for their loyalty once the Party took over, but some lied because they believed, despite their own experience, that the victory of the working class was the supreme good, a goal which sanctified all means. An ideal could not be defeated by mere facts and, anyway, whatever had not yet been accomplished would be accomplished in the future. All faces were turned to the distant horizon.

This frame of mind also helps to explain why, even years later, after all the horrors of Stalinism had become public knowledge, many old Communists could not give up their discredited faith. For them, the struggle for the ideal took on the meaning of a struggle for personal redemption. It was a victory over one's own smallness, an unselfish subordination of an individual's interests to the good of all society. To give up this ideal would be to disclaim the meaning of one's whole life.

This tendency toward self-sacrifice seemed to me extremely dangerous, even then. A good society is one in which everyone can live well, myself included. People who are ready to sacrifice their own well-being for some lofty goal are likely to exact a similar sacrifice from others who are not so willing. A political system which cannot function without martyrs is a bad, destructive system.

Those endless discussions about the economy! I could never understand the arguments properly. I only know that Rudolf and his friends were convinced that putting our economy back on its feet was their first and most important concern, and that it could be done only through socialist economics as they understood it. They certainly did not conceive of this process as a subordination of the Czech economic system to Soviet needs. Right from the start, while he was still working for the Czechoslovak Chamber of Industry, Rudolf concentrated on trade relations with the West, and later, as a Deputy Minister of Foreign Trade, he originated the so-called Dollar Offensive and other programs.

Today it is easy to look back, to judge, and to condemn, but I am sure that the mistakes that Rudolf and people like him made were errors of judgment, caused by flaws of intellect rather than flaws of character. The intentions were good, but of course intentions do not count. Sometimes evil intentions produce good results and good intentions produce the exact opposite—everything depends on the context. If the context is good, even the most ill-intentioned actions may be viewed in the light of history as forgiveable mistakes. Yet, when a man chooses a political system that turns out to be evil and incapable of correcting its errors, each one of his blunders may later be viewed as an unforgiveable crime. In a democracy, mistakes can eventually be rectified and people who perpetrate stupidity or even atrocities are regarded, with the passage of time, more with tolerance and pity than with hate. Two things about our situation in postwar Czechoslovakia should not be forgotten. First, no one except maybe the Soviet agents doubted that we would be able to run our own show, in a way that was quite different from the Russian totalitarian model. A "national road to socialism" was basic to our thinking, even to the thought of Klement Gottwald, the secretary general of the Czechoslovak Communist Party, who was encouraged to believe in it by Stalin himself. Marshall Tito, who had introduced a special brand of communism in Yugoslavia, was still a hero at the time, and following his example in our own country seemed a real possibility.

Second was the degree to which membership in the Communist Party, very much like belonging to a religious order, determined our lives. Party discipline demanded that we constantly analyze ourselves, our thoughts, our wishes, our inclinations—and whenever we discovered some discrepancy between the commandments of the Party and our own opinions, blame it on our bourgeois background, our antiquated reasoning, our intellectual decadence, or misguided education. When a person became a Communist he wanted to be a good Communist. We believed we were building on the ruins of a system that had failed but that had left a deep imprint on our way of thinking. We were, we thought, burdened with obsolete ideas, prejudices, weaknesses. Why had we surrendered to Hitler? Why had we allowed ourselves to be locked up in concentration camps and prisons? Because we were weak, spoiled, degenerate. If ever we wished to achieve anything, we had to change. Communism was the eternal ideal of humanity, we could not doubt the ideal, only ourselves.

It was an insidious process and as old as the world. Had it not been for the war and the overwhelming need for change, we would have seen through it easily. But when people come to reject everything and to doubt everything, it only means they doubt themselves and their ability to cope with the problems which face them—and the Party was prepared to provide the confidence that our war experiences had destroyed.

The horrors of the Occupation had taken their toll of everyone. Tens of thousands of Czechs had been imprisoned in jails and camps, had died in Gestapo torture chambers, had been executed. The Nazis had proclaimed the Slavs racially inferior, unfit for higher education, capable only of performing menial tasks for the master race. Universities had been closed during the war and young people forcibly drafted for hard labor in the most heavily-bombed regions of Germany. The result was a sudden loss of personal and national identity. Many good Czechs began to muse about who they really were, wondering if one could even speak of a Czech nation. After all, Czechoslovakia had only existed as a modern state since 1918.

The war had uprooted everything we thought we knew about life, people, history, ourselves; everything we had learned in school, from our parents, from books. The democratic government of Thomas Masaryk had instilled in us the certainty that some things could no longer happen. We had listened with only half an ear when our history teachers discussed torture or the persecution of innocent people. Those things could only have happened a long time ago, in the dark ages. When it happened in our time and in a form far worse than we could imagine, it felt like the end of the world. It seemed to us that we were witnessing a total break in the evolution of mankind, the complete collapse of man as a rational being.

For Czech Jews, the blow to identity was even worse, especially for those like Rudolf and myself whose families had considered themselves Czech for generations. Perhaps it seems odd that, before Hitler, it had never once occurred to me that I was different from other people. Rudolf once said, "When I was a child, I used to love all those books by Walter Scott and Alexandre Dumas, and I always imagined how I, too, would fight and fence and perform great deeds. It only occurs to me now that had I lived at that time I would have been rotting in some ghetto." After Hitler's Occupation, we were not Czechs anymore, not citizens, not students, not even human beings. Our value sank beneath the level even of cattle, because even cattle had to be fed. In Auschwitz, Jews became nothing more than pieces of junk that were burned in bulk in the incinerator.

Throughout history, there have been Jews who hated themselves for what they were made to suffer, for being the perennial focus of evil and violence wherever they were. Now we wondered, how much more difficult would it have been for Hitler had there been no Jews? How many Germans had joined the Nazi Party simply because it gave them the opportunity to snatch a share of Jewish property, to vent their frustrations? Maybe the Jews by their very existence had helped the Nazis to power more than anything else.

The Communists—even the Jews who were Communists—were in a vastly better psychological state. They suffered for an idea, for something they had chosen, not for what they were. Also, they knew what to expect from the fascists. The collapse of the old order only served to confirm their convictions. Their world was not turned upside down like ours, but moved quite logically in the direction in which they fully expected the bourgeoisie to lead it. The Nazis had always portrayed the Soviet Union as their most dangerous enemy. Eventually we came to believe that communism was the very opposite of Nazism, a movement that would restore all the values that Nazism had destroyed, most of all the dignity of man and the solidarity of all human beings. It came to seem that only another revolution could undo what the first had done.

That I myself did not succumb to the lure of ideology was certainly not because I was smarter than Rudolf but because I was a woman, a being much closer to reality and the basic things of life than he was. I was more interested in what was happening around me in the present, among the people I loved, than in the foggy spheres of ideology. Rudolf could decide on the basis of statistics—mostly falsified, or course—that under communism people lived a better and happier life. I saw from close-up and with my own eyes that this was not true.

A few months after the war was over, I took a trip to the forgotten little village near Benesov which was my father's birthplace. It was a long trip, first by train, then by bus, and I had plenty of time for memories.

My parents and I had once gone there in the winter to visit my grandmother. I had been quite small then, there had been lots of snow, and my grandmother's cottage had been warm and fragrant with burning wood. Her spotted puppy had played with me, newly-hatched chicks had peeped from a bin under her bed, and my grandmother had served us cake and huge walnuts. My father had taken me for a walk in the fields to show me where, as a child, he had once minded the geese. It was nearly dark when we returned; the pond was icing over and my grandmother was waiting for us on the porch, weeping because, while we were out, my father's sister had given birth to a baby girl on their farm not far away. Grandmother said that the baby was beautiful and that she would be called Marta like my mother. When Marta was only a few years old, she died in a concentration camp just like her parents, her brothers and sisters, and her grandmother.

I did not visit the farm. It had been taken over by strangers after the war. My grandmother's cottage looked neglected. Everything in it seemed even smaller than before. A kind old neighbor let me in and showed me where everything had happened. "See?" she said. "Here's where your grandmother set down her cup of coffee just before the Germans came. And here she sat with me for a while and I told her, 'Mrs. Bloch, don't be afraid . . .' "

I know there was nothing anyone could do. But they were taking away an 86-year-old grandmother to a horrible death, and the village where she had lived all her life, where everybody loved her, had just looked on. The only thing anyone had had to say was, "Mrs. Bloch, don't be afraid . . . "

I hesitated for a long time before I decided to sign the application for Party membership. I knew I would have trouble with the discipline. I hated meetings, and I was not at all interested in an active political life. I wanted to work, to study, to have a baby, to catch up on everything the war years had deprived me of. Why would I want to spend my evenings at meetings? All my life I had had trouble marching in closed ranks. The cheers of crowds, their shouted slogans, made me shiver. Right from the start, I took a dislike to the word "masses" which jumped out at me from every pamphlet I read. Whenever I saw or heard it, I had a vision of an endless flock of sheep, an undulating sea of bent backs and hung heads and the monotonous movement of chewing jowls. I hated the hysterical adulation of Stalin, the bombastic phrases of political oratory as well as the tinkle of medals and military decorations that covered the pot bellies of Soviet officers. But, I told myself, these were all unimportant details, quite suitable, after all, for the unsophisticated Russians with their history of czarist pomp.

In Czechoslovakia, it would all be different. We would not be building socialism in a backward society under conditions of imperialist intervention and inner turmoil, but at peace, in an industrially advanced country, with an intelligent, well-educated population. We would leap over a whole epoch.

Still, I did not feel like getting involved in politics. I kept saying to myself, "All I want is an ordinary, quiet life." But I came to realize that a quiet, simple life is neither ordinary nor easily attained. In order to be able to live and work in peace, to raise children, to enjoy the small and great joys life can offer, you must not only find the right partner, choose the right occupation, respect the laws of your country and your own conscience but, most importantly, you must have a solid social foundation on which to build such a life. You have to live in a social system with whose fundamental principles you agree, under a government you can trust. You cannot build a happy private life in a corrupt society anymore than you can build a house in a muddy ditch. You have to lay a foundation first.

Rudolf used to laugh and say, "I never thought you'd be one of those people who're neither hot or cold. If you sit on the fence now, you'll regret it for the rest of your life!"

That was the first mistake.

And then, "If you find you really don't belong in the Party, you can always resign."

That was the second mistake.

Finally one night I sat down at a Party meeting of the local organization with people who to this day call one another "Comrade." I rather liked that form of address. I liked the idea that people from different countries, speaking different languages, representing different races and cultures, could meet anywhere in the world and by calling one another "Comrade" recognize that although they had not met before and could not easily communicate, they shared certain things that they had chosen consciously and freely.

But that first meeting depressed me. Among those present was my old acquaintance from the Housing Authority, Mr. Boucek, along with another man who, it was said, had been jailed by the Germans for black marketeering and who was now styling himself as a former political prisoner, almost a national martyr, who had "fought against fascism." Most of the people present were at least twice my age and I was relieved when a young man with a full

68

beard arrived to lecture us on The Foundations of Marxism. His speech was a collection of platitudes and a few cautious, underhanded attacks on President Masaryk that made me furious. I was very troubled by the time he had finished, but then an older worn-out man, a bricklayer, got up to speak.

"This is all very nice," he said, "but let me tell you something about real life." He then talked about years of drudgery and poverty alternating with years of unemployment and misery, and finished by explaining what he expected from the future. He spoke slowly and groped for words, but his ideas seemed remarkably clear and to the point. On my way home, I said to myself, "One man like him is worth a hundred Mr. Bouceks and yes, yes, I am on the right side. Life is never simple. What is good is never entirely good, and evil is rarely evil through and through. I shall not permit myself to become discouraged."

Nonetheless, it was at this meeting that I first discovered that the Party did not draw its members solely from the ranks of the working class, the intellectuals, the antifascists, and the proletarians to whom our capitalist society had never given a chance. I think I would not be far wrong in saying that these people were a minority. Much later, even official spokesmen for the Party admitted that the Party had been infiltrated—but by whom?

There were collaborators who guessed that their dubious wartime activities could best be concealed under loud proclamations of loyalty to progress and socialism; there were black marketeers and crooks who hoped that a Party card would help them protect illegal earnings; there were corrupt bureaucrats and, of course, the vast army of the "humiliated and the wronged" who, due to incompetence or laziness, had never achieved anything and knew that in the Party their shortcomings could be turned into assets. They guessed, correctly, that in an organization that relied on strict, mindless discipline, mediocrity and the inability to think independently would prove to be the highest virtues.

For them, a totalitarian regime is ideal. The State and the Party think for them, take care of them, and give them the opportunity for revenge against the people they have always envied. In a totalitarian society there is a perpetual demand for petty informers and spies. Devotion to the Party, servility, and obedience richly compensate for intelligence, initiative, and honesty.

Other kinds of people also joined the Party. A Party card, in fact, soon became an essential credential for the large number of men jockeying for positions as the managers of nationalized companies, farms, and factories or as custodians of property left behind by evicted German and Czechoslovak emigrés, whose numbers were swelling. A few years later, I happened to visit a "comrade" who had just returned from a two-year stint in a border region. His apartment was like a museum. I had never before seen so many exquisite antiques and paintings in a private collection. He told me, "When I left Prague, I had nothing except a little suitcase in hand. And now just look!"

The most respected Party members were the prewar professional revolutionaries, people who had never in their life performed any useful work, but who had never missed a meeting or a strike. They also knew how to address the crowds in words and tones that would carry them, when the time came, to the highest positions in the Party and government.

It was not long before the concierges—the female custodians of most apartment houses in Czechoslovakia—became the backbone of the Party. For years they ruled with an iron fist not only over their own buildings but over entire streets. Their lives became an intoxicating orgy of spying and informing, which sometimes involved outright blackmail. Woe to the person who incurred their displeasure! Even the highest Party functionaries were careful not to drop cigarette ash on the staircase. Nor would an opportunity be missed to slip Comrade Concierge—who was usually also the local Party cell leader—some small gift. Just how important a position the concierges attained during the 1950s can be judged from a remark one of them made to me then.

"I think Comrade President Zapotocky must have been a concierge once himself," she said. "He has such sympathy for us!"

My dear woman, I thought to myself, Comrade President never in his life stooped to anything more strenuous than playing the accordion. At the time he was young, being a concierge was hard, honest work!

Yes, the Party was right. Many unsavory people had wormed their way into its ranks. Later though, we would wonder whether those people had not been the true core of the Party all along, whether the idealistic intellectuals and workers had not been the outsiders and infiltrators cited in Party propaganda. But even many of these honest idealists underwent a transformation when the Party seized power and began to dole out jobs. It is often said that power corrupts, but I think that what corrupted people in our country was not power alone but the fear that accompanied it. As soon as someone gained power, he became obsessed by the fear of losing it, because to lose power in our Communist society meant not a step down the social ladder to a former position, but a fall far below it. The higher one climbed, the harder one fell. The more one's power grew, the more dangerous its loss became, and the greater one's fear. And power sustained by fear is an infinitely cruel and dangerous combination.

I must confess, after saying all this, that for at least two years after the war was over, I did not pay much attention to public affairs; I had my hands full just finding my way back to everyday life. I spent whole months standing in lines in government offices waiting for official pieces of paper which would prove I was alive. The Germans had destroyed most of the archives; in order to get one new document, one needed to provide three old ones; in order to get hold of those three, one had to provide five others; and to find those five—it was endless. Nor was it easier to obtain other essential things: food, clothing, furniture. At the same time, I was standing on other lines in other offices, trying to find out what had happened to members of my family during the war. All my questions produced the same answers. Shot in Minsk. Perished in Maidanek. Died in Mauthausen. Deported to Auschwitz. Unaccounted for. Missing. Missing.

I would walk through the streets of Prague as though I were walking through a mine field where, with every step, the earth could open up under my feet. This was the street where I used to walk with my mother. This was the pastry shop to which my father would take me secretly on Sunday mornings for ice cream, and my mother would not know. This was the building where I first saw a flag with a swastika. This was the street through which our transport walked on the way to the train station, when people on the sidewalks stopped and took off their hats and the SS men shouted at them, *"Bewegung!* Move on or we'll take you with us!"

I was unable to take the advice of people who kept telling me that the only way back to life was to forget. I wanted to save everything, to cover up nothing, to pretty up nothing, to keep things inside me the way they had been, and to live with them. I wanted to live because I was alive, not just because by some accident I was not dead.

At the beginning of 1946, I found a job with a small prestigious publishing house as an art editor. I designed book jackets, assembled illustrations and reproductions, drew and painted, negotiated with writers and artists. I did things that fascinated me and that I thoroughly enjoyed. The publisher was an older gentleman, who taught me more about literature and art than I could have learned at school. We spent countless hours in museums and libraries and, at times, just rambling through the streets of the city where he knew every stone, the history of every building, sculpture, or painting.

I had plenty of time for these excursions because, even then, Rudolf was so involved in his work at the Institute for Industrial Development that he often came home late in the evening and then sat reading even later into the night. He was a lawyer, but now, with his usual diligence, he was studying economics, trying to make up for the time he had lost during the war. I grew accustomed to falling asleep in our tiny apartment with the desk lamp lighting up a stack of books on the table. To this day, when I think of Rudolf, I see him sitting there quietly, the dim light outlining his head.

We were both so wrapped up in our work that we paid little attention to what was going on around us. I only remember that wherever one turned in that year after the war, in homes or restaurants or even in the street, whenever two people began to talk, they immediately began to argue politics. Before the first election, in May of 1946, someone had scrawled on the fence near our house, "VOTE COMMUNIST OR AT LEAST SOCIAL DEMO-CRATS." The slogan amused me. I voted for the Social Democrats because that was the way my father had voted and because Rudolf's father had been a Social Democratic Party official. I was proud to carry on a family tradition. The Communists emerged strongest in the Parliament, even without my vote.

That autumn, I was thinking about enrolling at university, but I was pregnant and the doctor shook his head. "You have to take it easy," he said. "You're still weak. Why in God's name are all of you young people in such a hurry about everything?"

As it turned out, I had to spend the last few weeks of my pregnancy in bed. And then one Monday evening in February, a completely flustered Rudolf took me to the hospital. Until Thursday morning when my son was finally born, Rudolf wandered around the apartment and then through the streets and then through the hospital corridors, unkempt and in need of a shave, trailing rose petals from a bouquet that did not survive the waiting.

Ask me what was the most beautiful moment of my life and I can tell you exactly: it was when the nurse brought in my baby with his hair brushed into a cowlick, with long eyelashes, and eyebrows that looked painted on his soft little face, and said, "Here you have one handsome little boy!" The whole world lit up and burst into song, the bare hospital room filled with the scents of paradise, and suddenly my father and mother and grandmother appeared beside my bed, smiling. I pressed that little head close to me and said to myself, differently than I had ever said it before, "Life . . . life. . . . "

I resumed my work not long after that, but I worked at home so that I would not have to leave my baby. I withdrew completely into my private world. Outside it, things were changing, but I paid little attention. Rudolf would come home from work later and later. He regretted that he was not able to spend more time with his son but he seemed satisfied with his work and, when I look back on this time, it seems the most peaceful and contented period of our lives. Yet this would have been our last opportunity to gather our few belongings, bundle them up, and run as fast as we could from that light in the East that was rapidly becoming a conflagration.

Once or twice a week, Mrs. Machova would come to take the baby for a walk. I used those half days to take sketches I had finished over to my publisher, to bring home new work, and to take a look at life outside my home. One day at the end of February, 1948, I got ready to go out. I was in a particularly good mood. I put on my prettiest coat and a new hat and sauntered off through the streets of Prague. Toward the center of town, I came up against crowds of people, all marching in the direction of Old Town Square, and I thought sourly, Another demonstration! Why do people continue to find this kind of thing amusing? And in this freezing weather!

The intersection at the foot of St. Wenceslas Square was completely blocked by factory workers. The men stepped politely out of my way, calling out pleasant, flattering things in the charming way that men in Prague have. I smiled back at them and pushed my way through to Narodni Avenue.

As I entered the publisher's office, the old gentleman was standing at the window, looking down at the crowded street. He did not even turn around to greet me. He said, very quietly, "This is a day to remember. Today, our democracy is dying." I stood next to him, suddenly afraid. Out in the street, the voice of Klement Gottwald began thundering from the loudspeakers.

Every year, at the end of winter, when the air is still cold but already tinged with the promise of spring, I spend an afternoon with myself alone. Springtime has always been a time for remembrance.

There were the springtimes in Hut before the war, when people came out of their houses and into their gardens, airing out striped feather beds and turning the damp soil. Our neighbor, Grandfather Pleticha, never seemed to go back inside. Whenever I looked over into his garden I would see him standing there in an old short jacket, his hands in his pockets and a cloth cap above the weathered face of an old Czech puppet like the ones Matej Kopecky used to carve a century ago. I almost expected him to sink roots and start budding. From the corner window I had been used to seeing a bare slope covered with black trees. Then, one morning, I looked out and a green wind seemed to have blown through the forest. A few days later, the cobwebs of branches were hidden in a profusion of fresh, green leaves. People would stand outside their homes warming themselves in the sunshine and, year after year, they would say, "Isn't it beautiful?" as though they had never seen it before.

Then there were the springtimes in the Lodz Ghetto, where not a blade of grass would grow nor a single bird fly; the stench of quicklime used as disinfectant repelled all living things. But even in the Lodz Ghetto the wind would sometimes bring with it the smell of soil, of life. Far away somewhere, really just beyond the

Ghetto wall, there were fields where the Germans grew wheat.

Our last spring in Lodz, my father volunteered to work in those fields, and I worried about him. One day, I no longer remember how, I wangled a free afternoon and a pass to go after him. The sun was shining, and I saw him ahead of me, walking slowly behind the plow, bent under the strain. I saw for the first time how terribly he had aged, how pale he was, and how withered by hunger and humiliation. We stood together for a moment in the sunshine, and then my father took off his cap and said, shyly, "Now, in spring, my heart feels so heavy . . . " It was only many years later that I understood why he had chosen to do this work which was far more strenuous than what he had been doing before. Each day he had to walk a long distance before reaching the fields. Then, from dawn to dusk, he had to drag himself behind the plow, the heavy clogs on his feet sticking in the clay. But there he was alone with what he loved most, the freshly-turned earth, the open sky, the clean breeze. On the eve of his death, he had returned to those things from which he had come.

Springtimes in Prague—who could forget them? Forsythias on the Letna Plain. The flowering hills of Strahov. The chestnuts of Zofin. The gulls on Jirasek Bridge. There is no other city like Prague. It is not only the beauty of the buildings, of the towers and bridges, though it is that too. They rise up from the slopes and riverbanks in such harmony that it seems nature created them alongside its trees and flowers. But what is unique about Prague is the relation between the city and its people. Prague is not an uncaring backdrop which stands impassive, ignoring happiness and suffering alike. Prague lives in the lives of her people and they repay her with the love we usually reserve for other human beings. Prague is not an aggregate of buildings where people are born, work, and die. She is alive, sad, and brave, and when she smiles with spring, her smile glistens like a tear.

The spring of 1948 began dismally, with the death of Foreign Minister Jan Masaryk. He was the son of the first Czechoslovak president, Thomas G. Masaryk and, like his father, a symbol of the cultural values and humanistic traditions of our country. Many people believed that his presence in the new government—headed by the Communists—indicated that our road toward socialism might not, after all, deviate too far from the principles on which our Republic had been founded.

During the Nazi Occupation, Jan Masaryk had been Foreign Minister of the Czechoslovak government-in-exile in London. He had earned great respect from the Allied leaders and was enormously popular at home. Throughout the war he gave regular radio talks that were broadcast by the BBC; he had a way of giving people new hope and courage in the darkest moments of their lives, and they never forgot it. Whenever he appeared in public, people rallied around him and he exchanged jokes with them as though they were old friends.

Now, one morning less than a month after the Communist coup, his dead body was found on the pavement below the windows of his apartment in the Ministry of Foreign Affairs. Without disclosing the results of the autopsy or official investigation, the government announced that Jan Masaryk had killed himself in a fit of depression. Few people believed he was a suicide. Rumors of murder began to circulate immediately, and there were many theories about his death.

A good friend of ours, Pavel Kavan, was probably the last person to have seen Masaryk alive—except, possibly, for the unknown visitors who may have come later. Kavan, an official of the Foreign Ministry, said that Masaryk had seemed his usual self, neither unusually upset nor depressed, and had asked Kavan to return the next morning to pick up some documents. Another friend of ours, Stanislav Marek, who had known Masaryk for years, insisted that the Foreign Minister was prone to severe depressions, and that no one who really knew him well was surprised at his suicide.

The mystery of Jan Masaryk's death was never solved. But whether he had become too great an obstruction to Soviet plans and was consequently put out of their way by experts, or whether he took his own life out of despair over the future of his country, one thing was clear: the Communist coup or, as the Party came to call it, "Victorious February," was the cause of his death.

Three or four months later, over dinner one evening, Rudolf told me that he had been offered the position of cabinet chief in the Ministry of Foreign Trade. The prospect scared me. By that time we all realized that the coup had been a fundamental upheaval, with tremendous consequences for the whole country, a revolution that some people had met with cheers and others with dread. Many of our friends had left Czechoslovakia for lives abroad; others were staying but lived with a feeling of constant apprehension. Everything around us was falling apart or being torn down. I knew that the great change I had read about in those pamphlets had finally come, but I wondered whether it would be a change for the better.

I wanted Rudolf to wait a while before he said yes or no to the Ministry. What if things took a direction he could not support? What if all that idealism should fail in practice? As an ordinary Party member he could, perhaps, voice disagreement, resign or protest. But I knew enough about Party practice by then to realize that the people who occupied positions in the higher echelon of government or Party had little margin for dissent. "Whoever is not with us is against us," ran the slogan: either one belonged, body and soul, to the Party, or one was considered a traitor.

Luckily, Rudolf himself said he did not want the job. He was not suited for it. He was satisfied with what he was doing. He still had a lot to learn. He had already turned down the offer. He wondered why he had even been considered for such an important job—an inexperienced young man like himself, a recent Party member who had never held any political office or performed any Party function.

Two days later, we were expecting Otto and Milena for dinner, after which we were to go to the theater. Rudolf arrived at the last minute. He said that his refusal to take the job had been rejected. The Party had officially ordered him to accept. Party superiors had explained that his work at the Institute had been carefully watched, that his qualifications were outstanding, and

78

that his knowledge of foreign languages was very useful. The Party needed him. The Party had decided.

Now the choice was simple, Rudolf said. He could either accept the position of cabinet chief in the Ministry of Foreign Trade or resign from the Party and turn his back on everything he believed in. I began to object to this line of reasoning, but Rudolf stopped me.

"You see?" he said. "That's just like us! As long as everything's on paper, in theory, we can get excited. But when the time comes to act, we lose our nerve! Who knows if it's the right thing to do? But don't ask me to step aside and spend the rest of my life blaming myself for cowardice. You can never get anywhere if you're afraid of making a mistake. I'm convinced we're capable of building a fairer and, in the end, a freer society. I have to accept the responsibility that goes along with that conviction. I know you think we'll have the same terror here as in Russia after the Revolution. But if you took the time to study these things, you'd see that the two countries offer entirely different conditions. Developments here will be totally different. Everything depends on getting good people in decisive positions so that we don't waste energy and resources and so that we don't hurt anyone."

I remember arguing that, as cabinet chief, Rudolf would be nothing more than the foreign minister's errand boy, forced to carry out policies made without his participation. "Experts like you will have no influence on actual decisions," I said. "But you'll be made the scapegoat for anything that goes wrong. Don't you know it's always the second or third man down the line who makes the mistakes? It's only the top guy who gets the recognition for something that works!"

"I don't care about recognition," Rudolf said. "Besides, it's clear I'll only be there for the interim. I'm basically still a man of the old order. In a year or two, when enough young workers finish up their education, I'll be glad to give the job up and get back to my books. You know, that's probably my one real qualification for this job: I'm not interested in furthering my own career; I'll do honest work."

Suddenly I was overcome by all the tensions of the previous weeks and burst into tears. The doorbell rang just then, and Otto and Milena came in. Rudolf explained to them what was going on and Milena threw up her hands.

"For God's sake!" she said. "I've known you since first grade. I've lived through all kinds of horrors with you. And the first time I see you cry is when your husband makes it to the top! Have you gone crazy?"

We did go to the theater that evening and, for a short while, I pushed my worries aside. We did not talk about the job anymore after we returned home. We lay in bed in the dark for a long time, each listening to the other's breathing, each knowing that the other was wide awake. Finally, Rudolf said, "I know that the next few years won't be easy but, after that, if we do our job well, people will be happier and better off. Isn't that worth a try?"

I felt the touch of his fingers at the corners of my mouth.

"Please," he said. "Smile just a little."

What I remember most vividly from this period following the coup is a feeling of bewilderment, of groping in the dark that was doubly oppressive because the darkness was not only outside but inside me as well. How could we have been so credulous? so ignorant? It seems that once you decide to believe, your faith becomes more precious than truth, more real than reality.

My world began to change right away, the day the newspapers announced Rudolf's nomination to his new post in the Ministry of Foreign Trade. I went for my weekly appointment with the hairdresser. He was a fine fellow and I had always been casually friendly with him and his staff. While Mr. Oldrich dried my hair, one of his apprentices usually played with the baby or took him for a walk in his stroller. This time, no one greeted me with a joke or a smile. Instead, the entire staff stopped what they were doing and stood at attention. My hairdresser himself helped me off with my coat, hung it up, and started dancing around me, offering all kinds of essences and rinses—the same ones he used to dismiss, saying, "Stay away from this junk!" When I blurted out, "What's the matter with you?" he answered, "Nothing. But everything's the matter with you. You can't treat a highly-placed person like your-self as though you've herded geese with her all your life!"

That was the first indication of things to come. I had to become accustomed to the fact that, for everyone but a handful of my old friends, I ceased to be a human being. Instead, I became an object of envy, hate, suspicion, or obsequious deference. In the years that Rudolf would hold his job at the Ministry, I would not succeed in making a single friend among the comrades or their wives, and I think that fact illuminates the nature of that time. When ideology takes the front seat, human relations are pushed aside. When every action and thought is geared to the building of a new society, there is little room left for feelings. Feelings are tricky anyway, hard to channel, hard to control: they are distractions from work and con-structive effort, better avoided. The only feelings one can safely enjoy are love for the Party and hearty solidarity with one's com-rades. Of course, even here caution is advisable; one should thor-oughly examine a comrade before bestowing upon him one's trust. Only the Party is worthy of unquestioning devotion. I remember an actress, an outstanding artist, who declared to me that anyone whose eyes did not grow moist at the mention of Lenin's name was not worthy of standing on the stage of the National Theater.

At about that time, one of Rudolf's colleagues came to visit us and the conversation turned to precisely these matters. "Rudolf, you know how much I like you," the man said, "and that I consider you a good friend. But if I ever found out you had done anything to hurt the Party, I'd turn against you in a minute and do my best to make you pay for it."

I remembered this statement a few months later when this same man began to turn up at our home, terrified. He told us he was being followed everywhere by a black Tatra police limousine, and begged us to let him sit down and relax with us for a few moments. He was one of the first prominent Party members to be arrested, and I felt sorry for him, but since he had always seemed a bit enigmatic to me and capable of anything, I was prepared to believe that he might have been involved in some unsavory activities.

About two months after the coup, an older woman whom I did

not know called at our apartment. She said she had heard that we wished to move. That was true. Our little hole in the wall had been bursting at the seams ever since the birth of our son. She offered me an apartment in her house in the Letna district which had been left vacant by some people who had emigrated. I liked the place even though it was none too spacious and was quite expensive. The rooms were still filled with the belongings of their former tenants.

I found the family's former housekeeper in the kitchen. A fat, simple girl who was helping the landlady clean out the apartment, she was sitting over a cup of coffee as I came in. "Lady don't take this place," she whispered to me. "It's jinxed. First there were Jews here—they all died in the camps. The Germans who took the apartment from them got out in the nick of time—the neighbors would have lynched them! And now the people I worked for ran away with only their knapsacks on their backs. Nobody ever leaves this place in an ordinary way."

The apartment was convenient and we needed a place where three people could live. I decided that we would take it.

My social obligations began right after we moved in. I have little interest in entertaining, but I was willing to do it for Rudolf's sake. Even today I feel gloomy when I remember the dinners and receptions we had to attend as part of our duty to the Party. The men, most of them as fanatically devoted to their work as Rudolf, used these occasions as work meetings and left us, their wives, to amuse ourselves as best we could. I think most of the wives suffered the same agonies of boredom I did.

The wives fell into two categories: the daughters of the working class and those with a bourgeois past similar to my own. The first group, secure in their proletarian origins, were self-assured, loud, and stolid, confident that anything they said or did could be justified by their background. The second group was constantly on guard, each woman afraid of making some politically inappropriate slip, of appearing too intellectual or uncommitted and, thereby, shaming herself as well as damaging her husband's career. It often happened that, once we had exhausted the safe topic of children, we stood or sat around for hours in cramped silence, maintaining smiles that made our face muscles ache, nodding at the chatter of our working class comrades. Once, after I had been standing in a corner with the wife of one of our leading economists for an hour without exchanging a single word, she could stand the boredom no longer and blurted out, "Have you seen anything interesting at the theater lately?" Then, appalled by the possible ramifications of what she had said, she babbled, "Oh, please forgive me for asking such a bourgeois question!"

In fact, our lack of political awareness soon became so obvious to the authorities that the Party arranged for a special series of lectures on Marxism for us. Many of the wives would bring along their knitting or darning to these talks, to demonstrate their positive attitude toward manual labor.

Those receptions! Perhaps the most startling thing about them was their lavishness. Tables groaned under the weight of rare delicacies at a time when ordinary people were still living on rations. A *nouveau-riche* snobbery thrived among those very same people who made the most of their working class origins and proletarian principles, and who ruled in the name of workers and farmers. One of these comrades reprimanded me one evening for wearing too simple an evening gown to a reception given by Ambassador Konstantin Zorin. Attendance at Soviet receptions, she said, demanded full formal attire—even though clothing and fabric were still being rationed in Czechoslovakia.

Rudolf had bought a used car that he loved to drive and in which we sometimes arrived at these receptions. This, too, became the occasion for an official rebuke: first for the fact that we chose to arrive in an old car, and second for the fact that Rudolf himself was at the wheel. The new elite considered nothing short of a chauffeur-driven limousine to be appropriate.

I found myself in a cross fire. On the one hand I was constantly and disapprovingly monitored by our concierge and my neighbors, who discussed my every step and once even called a meeting to discuss my shockingly unproletarian style of dress. On the other hand, there were the equally stringent eyes of my comrades in the elite, who were drowning in tasteless luxuries made possible by special ration cards that Rudolf refused to accept. I resolved the problem, probably badly, by ignoring both groups.

The street on which we now lived had a peculiar character. During the war, many Germans had taken over its large expensive apartments. After liberation, they had been superseded by a strange assortment of newly-rich Czechs who had joined the Party out of sheer expediency. Few actual workers lived on our street, but there were several shopkeepers and tradesmen who evidently believed that, in order to hold on to their livelihoods, they had to pose as hard-core Bolsheviks, aglow with class enthusiasm. It happened at almost every local Party meeting that some woman who owned a laundry or a grocery store would rise to her feet and declare ingenuously, "Comrades, if you only knew how dearly I love our Party," and then sit down again.

Once, just before May Day, someone inquired shyly whether it would not be wasteful to squander miles of good fabric and countless pieces of lumber on May Day parade decorations when these scarce commodities could surely be put to better use in our post-war economy. This brought the owner of the local dairy shop to his feet. "What's this?" he demanded. "Who is it that dares to suggest that anything for the glory of the Party is wasteful? I say, comrades, let's have even bigger and better decorations—cost be damned! We'll show the capitalists!" But all this bluster did not help him; his store was nationalized just a few months later anyhow.

The chairman of our local Party organization was a strange, stunted character with a long, horse face, and he had a plump wife who also vaguely resembled a horse. Both were endowed with a pathological venomous curiosity and spent their days and nights probing into the most intimate details of the lives of the people who lived on our street, Communists and non-Communists alike. This opportunity for snooping into the lives of other people was, I think, something that attracted many to the local Party organization. Gossip had become a virtue and an obligation. A Communist was duty-bound to be aware of everything taking place around him, and I knew many people who spent whole days standing in the street or by their windows so as not to miss a thing.

It may seem strange but, at the time, these things did not upset me very much. They made the atmosphere unpleasant, but it all seemed more ridiculous than ominous. By then, I had few illusions left about people, and I was not about to let my life be soured by such trivia. They were far outweighed by Rudolf's conviction that we were on the right track and that no obstacle was insurmountable.

Occasionally, people came to us for help, complaining of an injustice. Mostly these were older people, tradesmen whose shops had been confiscated but who were not eligible for social security since they had been self-employed. Now they were looking for other jobs or for pensions, and frequently Rudolf was able to help them. There were others who came because they wished to leave the country, but these Rudolf could not help. The borders had been closed in 1948 after the coup. Of all the injustices and inanities perpetrated during those years, the closing of the borders was among the worst. Why not let people leave? Why keep them against their will? One comrade from the Ministry of Foreign Affairs explained that it was only a temporary measure. "The Republic can't afford to lose members of its labor force," he said. "For many people, the decision to leave is rash. They don't understand the situation and are prone to an entirely unjustified panic. Once they realize they have nothing to be afraid of, they'll be glad they stayed. Then we'll open the borders up again and people will travel where they want."

For many people, especially young people, 1948 was a year which also saw the realization of long-held hopes. There was more than enough work for everyone. Even housewives began to look for jobs—some out of necessity but others for the satisfaction of taking part in public life. People worked enthusiastically, even on holidays and Sundays, and many spent their evenings studying. They made plenty of money, often more than they could spend, and bought up everything in sight.

Tax-supported national health care was instituted, as were old age pensions and free vacation plans for workers. The nationalization of private businesses was causing some bad blood, of course, but we were told that this was to be expected; it was a difficult step that was imperative for the expansion of our economy. Whenever I looked out the window of a train at the landscape striped with tiny privately-owned fields I had to admit it was true—private farming had no future. No one, at the time, could have imagined how the crude, ruthless process of collectivization would damage our agriculture, that it would be fifteen or twenty years before the new nationalized farms would break even.

Sometime in 1950, a friend whom we called Karlicek came from the country to visit us in Prague. Before the coup, Karlicek had owned a large farm not far from Prague which was now nationalized. He was a good man and a superb farmer whom the villagers liked and welcomed as a friend whenever he came to visit and to observe the downhill slide of his once-prosperous farm. He stormed into our apartment one day and started shouting at Rudolf, "When one of my cows produced less than ten liters of milk, I sent her to the slaughterhouse because she consumed more than she produced. And you know what they're doing now? They give a medal to a cow that's producing *four* liters! You idiots!"

At about the same time, Prague wits were beginning to define socialism as a system designed to successfully resolve problems that could never arise under any other political system.

Yet Rudolf plunged into his work with such enthusiasm that some of it rubbed off on me. The people with whom he worked seemed equally industrious and intelligent and, as far as I could see, their mission of developing trade relations with the West had started off auspiciously. I was particularly pleased with the help Czechoslovakia was extending to Israel and the fact that Rudolf was instrumental in that program. But, other than that, I knew few specifics about Rudolf's work. Everything was Secret and Top-Secret and, after a while, I stopped asking questions about his projects. His world, symbolized by the briefcase that no one was allowed to touch, was becoming closed to me.

Rudolf worked late almost every night and was often summoned to the Ministry on Sundays while I spent whole afternoons in the park, wheeling my baby in his carriage, envying the happy family clusters around me. Before Rudolf had taken the job at the Ministry we had never missed a good play, and both of us, especially Rudolf who was a gifted violinist, loved music. Now when I bought tickets to the theater or for a concert, he almost always called at the last minute to say he could not get away in time. Our child was growing up hardly knowing his father.

Once, I managed to talk Rudolf into taking a week-end trip to the mountains. We were both avid skiers and there is nothing more beautiful than our mountains in the winter. But that Saturday the weather was against us. Barely a few miles out of Prague we got into a snowstorm and, by the time we reached the foothills, it was snowing so hard that we could not tell the road from the middle of a field. We moved at a snail's pace, looking out a half-open door, trying to guess where we were. Suddenly Rudolf turned to me and said in amazement, "Would you believe it? For almost an hour now, I haven't thought of foreign trade!"

Much later, I came to wonder whether this insane work load was not intentional. No one who held a responsible government position had a free moment in which to verify how his work affected the everyday life of the ordinary person. Government and Party functionaries socialized only with each other; they saw only each other at their conferences, meetings, and councils; they judged the state of the country only from official papers and reports which were often inaccurate or completely fake. Because each of them concentrated so intensely on his own limited area of work, they lost perspective and any genuine understanding of the real needs and wishes of the people. Even if they had occasion to speak with someone outside their circle, that person usually did not feel free to complain or criticize. Rudolf was not the kind of man who inspired fear, but his belief in the rightness of what he was doing moved people, silenced them and, eventually isolated him.

Gradually, I became Rudolf's only link with the ordinary world. Except for one fierce argument over a serve I had bungled during a volley-ball match two weeks after our wedding, we had never had any of those personal conflicts that add zest to the best of marriages. Now we wasted most of the precious time we spent together in bitter, useless arguments about the political situation— useless, because Rudolf considered his statistics far more reliable than my day-to-day experiences and complaints, which he dismissed as narrow and prejudiced. People were well-off, he argued. Poverty was a thing of the past. No one was out of work. Yes, here and there, something went wrong. But everything would be straightened out eventually. Give it time. "Just wait a few years. You'll see."

Late one night, the wife of the grocer at whose store my mother used to shop before the war knocked at our apartment door. In tears, she told us that the police had barged into their apartment, turned everything upside down, and had taken her husband away without telling her where or why. The grocer, a kind, jolly, very fat man, was also a well-known black marketeer, so it did not seem impossible to us that he had been arrested for good reason. But why had it been done in gangster fashion? Rudolf promised to find out what he could, and the woman went home somewhat relieved. The following day we found out that many small shopkeepers and artisans had been dragged away at the same time and that no one knew where they were or what they were accused of having done. Many of them waited in jail for months before they were finally tried by People's Tribunals whose decisions were based not on our established legal system but on "class feeling," and whose sentences were meted out in a completely haphazard way.

The grocer's arrest was the first event that jarred Rudolf as much as it did me. He was able to ascertain the whereabouts of the unlucky grocer after just a few days, and to inform his wife of them. But that was all. I think it was the first time that it dawned on Rudolf how precarious the rule of law and the dispensation of justice had become in our country.

By this time, late in 1949, the Soviet Union had become our model. Yugoslavia had been officially declared a preserve of spies and traitors, and all our Ministries were being reorganized along more centralized lines. Rudolf's job at the Ministry of Foreign

Trade had been eliminated; he was now a deputy minister, in charge of trade with the West. The official newspapers declared that the class struggle was escalating but that we were not to worry since the Party was ever alert and watchful. Movie houses were showing films that featured saboteurs and spies trying to undermine the unity of the working class; bookstores were stocked with books about the Great Conspiracy against the Party and Comrade Stalin. We read about the uncanny cleverness of the enemy who was adept at disguising himself before the closest of colleagues and even his own family.

No one was, by then, repeating the old slogan that any person who meant well would have an opportunity to develop his abilities and take part in building socialism. The Party had given up on persuasion and had instead taken up cadre evaluation. People sat up till late at night filling out forms that probed into the lives of third-generation ancestors. What a person knew, what kind of work he could do and how well, became irrelevant. The things that mattered were class-consciousness and class origin, attitude toward the New Order, and, most of all, devotion to the Soviet Union.

The rationale was not at all complex. Every individual is a product of his class, education, upbringing, and environment. If your father had owned a notions store or a peanut stand, you were clearly the product of a private enterprise mentality and, therefore, could not be trusted. The way in which backgrounds were evaluated at the time sometimes produced comic results. I knew a man who, before the war, had owned a tiny yard-goods store in a small village and who had barely managed to feed his family. His shop had been nationalized and, as a former member of the petty bourgeoisie, he had been sent to work in a factory by way of reeducation. From that moment on, his children could proudly write "worker" in every questionnaire which asked for their father's occupation and were thereby easily able to acquire positions and salaries of a kind that their bourgeois father had never dreamed possible. On the other hand, the son of Party ideologue and Minister Ladislav Stoll was, at first, refused admission to university and advised to go work in the coal mines since, as the son of a government official, he was not of worker or peasant origin.

In the summer of 1949, Rudolf was preparing to go to London as head of a delegation that was to negotiate a trade agreement with England. It was an extremely difficult, precarious enterprise. The Soviet Union had, earlier, prohibited Czechoslovakia from participating in the Marshall Plan and viewed with suspicion all our dealings with the West. Any concessions that Rudolf made to the demands of the British could later be construed by the Party as intentional sabotage of our national interests or, at best, as incompetence. I did not know any details of the situation; I only saw that Rudolf was even more thoughtful and concerned than usual. Then, one evening, he came home in an altogether different mood. He said he had been assured a completely free hand in the upcoming negotiations and that the Party would consider any accord a success.

Rudolf flew to London and then returned twice to Prague for consultations. I was happy to see him, but we did not talk much; his thoughts were elsewhere. When the trade agreement was finally signed and Rudolf returned home, President Gottwald summoned him to his private apartment, embraced him, and congratulated him on a job superbly done. On the side of the British the agreement had been negotiated by Harold Wilson, who later became a Labour prime minister; it was considered an important asset in the development of our trade with the West. Rudolf, who had returned home exhausted, could finally relax.

The autumn that year was beautiful and warm, and Rudolf was so tired that I managed to talk him into taking a week's vacation. We loaded the car and, without any specific destination in mind, set out for a drive through Bohemia. But the vacation was not a success. The beauty of the landscape, calm and restful, only intensified the apprehension which, by that time, almost never left me. For hours, we sat side by side in silence, but not in the way we had so often done in the past when we had felt so close to one another that there was no need to talk. Now we were silent out of fear that anything we said would betray our anxiety. I watched

90

Rudolf's tired profile as he drove and thought, what a wretched wife I am; instead of giving him support, I'm always pulling him back, discouraging him.

We had put the top of the car down and were driving down deserted tree-lined country roads. On both sides, the sloping fields were engraved with the dark parallel lines of freshly-plowed furrows. I clearly remember one part of the road where the crowns of tall old trees intertwined above us like a shimmering golden net cast over the blue sky. I threw my head back, the wind hit my face, and suddenly I was struck with such a sure sense of impending disaster that it was as though we were hurtling down the leafy tunnel straight into destruction, as though death itself was waiting at the end of that peaceful country road. To this day my heart sinks whenever I look up in a car and, instead of the sky, see a vault of branches which the trees fold over my head in a gesture of despair.

On the third day of our vacation, we reached the village where my old friend Martin, a former partisan who had helped hide me during the last months of the war, was staying in a cottage by a lake. We spent the night there, the water quietly splashing under our windows as though we were sleeping in a boat.

The next morning Rudolf went for a walk in the woods, and Martin suggested that the two of us go out in the rowboat. When we had reached the middle of the lake, Martin stowed the oars and said soberly, "Now listen: you have to do everything possible to get your husband to leave his job. If you can't find any other way, cause some scandal so that they fire him! If he stays there, he's done for, that's for sure. When I talk to him, I can't understand how someone so smart can be so blind. The more he works, the better he does, the worse it'll be. Everything he achieves will be turned against him. We're running on the Russian track now and all the stops will be the same. They'll start looking for scapegoats any day, especially among those people who have the genuine interests of the country at heart. Rudolf is made-to-order for the role."

That lonely rowboat in the middle of the lake, that terse, serious voice—it took me back to years before. Martin was not making small talk on an autumn morning. This was not a friendly warning, but an order from a commander of the partisans.

"What about you, Martin?" I asked. "Are you looking out for yourself? Or are you mixed up in something again? Be careful! This isn't Nazi Germany. It won't be over in six years. This time you don't stand a chance."

People like Rudolf, who staked their lives on their convictions, did not do so without deliberation. Theirs was an arduously-won faith that could not easily be shaken. They ascribed the steadily deteriorating quality of life in Czechoslovakia after the coup to the incompetence of the people on top, people who had been chosen for their positions because of their working-class background, and who often lacked both experience and professional qualifications. They were incapable—it was argued—of mastering the intensifying conflicts within our society which, in turn, were caused by increasing international tension. As late as 1950, I would hear people say, "The Soviets should take the situation in hand. If Stalin only knew what was going on here, he would step in and put an end to this mess!" Once the wife of a prewar Communist who had been arrested a few weeks before came to me for advice and actually wondered out loud whether she should turn to the Soviet Embassy for help.

Those were the days of the Cold War. The Iron Curtain had come down and had cut us off from the rest of the world. Our newspapers printed every word that Soviet Foreign Minister Andrei Vishinsky uttered in his endless speeches at the United Nations but never mentioned that anything was said in reply. All we ever read about the West was news of strikes which, apparently, took place all the time and everywhere, and of the persecution of Communists. Once I was listening to the news on the radio and caught the word "Netherlands." I pricked up my ears but the news item was only that the Soviet Folk Dance Collective had enjoyed a great success in Amsterdam. That was the only bit of news from the West that we had had for months.

The few books by Western authors that were being translated at the time—mainly works of fiction by Howard Fast, Stephen Heym, and Jack Lindsay—gave such a grim picture of life in the West that we could only conclude that the Party was right, that the West had reached the terminal stages of moral and economic decay.

Very few people listened to foreign broadcasts such as Radio Free Europe or the BBC, partly out of fear, but mainly because the broadcasts were so effectively jammed that it was almost impossible to understand what was being said. Occasionally someone would catch a few words out of context, surmise the rest, and pass it on. That first bit became further distorted by repetition until people dismissed it with a wave of the hand, "Now you see how they lie!"

We believed that another world war was just around the corner and that police surveillance had become the rule all over the world— not only in our own country. Throughout 1950 and 1951, the officially-proclaimed, ideologically-justified class war within Czechoslovakia intensified, and most of us believed that it was a necessary evil. We all knew that the regime had many internal enemies, that the black market and all sorts of other rackets were flourishing. When the arrests first started, it was generally assumed that the accused were all guilty of something. Few people at that time chose to believe that there was something basically wrong with our judicial system. After all, the accused almost invariably confessed.

I remember the amazement with which I read reports of the trial of a group of priests accused of treason. Not only did they promptly confess to every crime with which they were charged, but they spoke like lecturers on Marxism, formulating their testimony in the purest Party jargon. One comrade explained the phenomenon to me in this way: while interrogating the accused, our investigators sought to reeducate them, and to clarify the goals and principles of the Party in such a manner that the accused would themselves understand how and why they were guilty. Such was the force of the Party's truth, the comrade insisted, that, in the end, it won over even the enemy. Every government had an obligation to defend itself against its enemies. Just look at America and Joseph McCarthy's witch hunts! It was only when someone we knew well was arrested, someone we knew could not possibly have been guilty of any crime, that we began to pull our heads out of the sand.

At first we would say, there must be some mistake. He'll be held for questioning and then let go. It will all be clarified in no time.

Then, when the person was not immediately released: I've known this man for years. He's no traitor. Something shady's going on here. It must be some kind of conspiracy master-minded by the West. They want to weaken the Party and cast suspicion on our best people. It won't work. Truth will out.

Finally, we would say nothing at all. Stunned, terrified silence was our only response. Only then did it begin to dawn on a few people that we were, in fact, the victims of a conspiracy, but hardly of one that was directed by the West.

It was not until years later, when some of the people arrested in the early 1950s were released and cautiously "rehabilitated," their innocence reluctantly proclaimed by the Party, that the whole picture became clear. One day in 1956, at a time when the "rehabilitated" had begun to be seen in the streets, I met my friend Pavel Eisler, who had never formally joined the Party but who had belonged to the earliest group of its enthusiasts and had worked in the Office of the President until 1951. He stopped short when he saw me, so upset that he could not say a word. For a few moments we just stood there staring at each other.

Then he said, "I just saw a man from our office who was arrested in 1950. At the time I was so surprised. I thought: Who would have guessed? He seemed such a decent fellow, yet he was a traitor. Now, after six years, he's out of jail. And he was completely innocent! He looks twenty years older, his hair is gray, his teeth were all knocked out. And when they were taking him away, all I did was shake my head and wonder. Can you believe that? I didn't even feel sorry for him! My God, what idiots we were!"

That's what we were, the worst kind of idiots.

The more dignified and humane an image of man was drawn by the Party, the less did men themselves come to mean in society. The better and more joyous our lives appeared on the pages of the newspapers, the sadder they were in reality. The housing shortage became desperate. Often two or three families were crammed into one apartment, deprived of all comfort and privacy. In order to make room for the young, many retired people were forcibly moved to the country, sometimes into summer cottages situated in remote areas and unfit for year-round habitation. Many elderly people who did not belong to the working class were denied their old-age pensions and lived in dismal poverty.

There were endless lines in front of stores. There were shortages of practically every household staple. Every few months, there were new rumors about an upcoming currency devaluation. People would panic, buying up anything they could find. The chaotic economy and the constant barrage of ideology drained all pleasure from honest work. Almost everyone was moonlighting for an often semi-legal second income and put in an appearance at his regular place of work just to rest up. Nationalized enterprises went steadily downhill. Our lives, permeated by insecurity, became hopeless drudgery. Suspicion became so prevalent that no one trusted anyone else. The enemy was no longer outside but within the Party as well; not even the comrades dared to speak out. Our whole world began to disintegrate. Even Rudolf's optimism was gone by 1951, replaced by a driven self-punishing toil.

The publisher for whom I had worked was no longer in business. The old gentleman, embittered but philosophical, had decided to retire. I had found another position, as an art director in a newly-organized publishing house for scientific literature where, for the first time, I became acquainted with a socialist enterprise.

The other editors were all young, almost all Party members,

96

and their zeal knew no bounds. Most of them were still university students who spent their Sundays and holidays on labor brigades; they had each day planned down to the minute in order to manage it all. Unfortunately, none of them had the slightest idea about managing a publishing house and, despite their enthusiasm, they made such a mess of it that within two years the enterprise went bankrupt and was closed.

It was while working with them that I first understood what a committed collective was like and, at first, their dutifulness, their idealism, and their naive belief in the infallibility and virtual holiness of the Party stunned me. I could not understand how people so young could give up the pleasures of private life and identify completely with a prescribed mode of thought. No matter what happened, my colleagues never doubted that what the Party did, it did well. None would ever dream of complaining about the endless meetings and conferences. They obeyed the arbitrary directives issued by the comrades of the Central Committee which supervised our activities to the letter; they uttered the names of these comrades with awe. In this exemplary collective I, for the first time, heard this admonition routinely delivered to the more frivolous members of the Party: "Another date? Aren't you ashamed to waste time dating when there's a war on in Korea?"

Only two people at the house did not fit this mold. One was the editor-in-chief, Jiri Stano, a young man of rather dim intellect and minimal industry. His directives were largely limited to invitations to his favorite editors to join him for a swig of liquor that he kept in a large bottle in the drawer of his desk. He was, some months after my arrival, relieved from his duties and promoted to a loftier position. After 1968, he became a pillar of the Party daily *Rude Pravo*—the Russian occupation version—where his articles suggested that he had not overcome his intellectual limitations but had merely learned to make better use of them.

The second misfit in the collective was Pavel Kovaly, who seemed to be far more interested in skiing and canoeing than in Party life. He soon became my trusted ally and developed an admirable resourcefulness in extricating us from Party meetings. He often walked me home from work, and became acquainted with Rudolf. Whenever we happened to have a free hour or two, he would come by our apartment for a bit of conversation or a game of chess with Rudolf.

At the time there was a film being shown in Prague which Comrade Stano liked to discuss, with deep emotion, calling it the pinnacle of Socialist Realism and a masterful reflection of Soviet life. It was called *Cossacks from the Kuban* and it featured buxom young women and handsome young men turning hay and harvesting wheat to the accompaniment of a four-part chorus of socialist work songs. Perfect harmony reigned in this classless paradise and one of our editors, in what was obviously a fit of temporary insanity, remarked that the film had struck her as just another grade-B operetta. The remark rendered the collective speechless. The editor was asked to conduct a self-critique at the next meeting and, with the help of all the comrades, to correct her erroneous views. She was asked to continue correcting them for some ten more meetings and, had it not been for the complete exhaustion of everyone concerned, she would still have been doing penance in 1968.

My colleague Borivoj, the other staff artist with whom I shared the room designated as a studio, was an exceptionally nice, friendly young man who, among other things, was a member of the Folk Song and Dance Ensemble. He had gone on tour with the Ensemble several times and had also visited the Soviet Union. He was always bursting with energy that, oddly enough, resulted in very little actual work accomplished, but he was very helpful to me. He saw to it that we had all the supplies we needed, he ran errands, he tended the bulletin board, he kept an eye on the level of my political awareness, and he amused me. Borivoj liked to recall his tours of Russia, to describe the hospitality of the people he had met, their friendliness, the ancient railroad cars that were maintained with such touching care, the godforsaken train stations in the steppe surrounded by beds of red flowers.

We were getting along wonderfully until the day when he rushed into our studio with a cardboard folder from which he produced a color reproduction of an oil painting that would shortly be seen all over Prague.

"Well? What do you think?" he asked.

The print showed a mass of clouds which were colored a vivid pink—it was hard to tell whether by sunrise or sunset. Against this gaudy backdrop stood a violet tractor dwarfed by the highly idealized figure of the beloved father of all proletarians, Iosif Vissarionovich Stalin. The effect was overwhelming. Each detail of Stalin's body was so painstakingly executed that you felt like moving over and letting him jump out of the picture.

"Good grief," I moaned. "What unbelievable *kitsch!*"

Unable to take my eyes off the picture, I realized only a few moments later that my colleague had not responded to my comment. When I looked over at him, I saw that his face had turned the same hue of pink as the clouds of the print and that he was gasping. Finally, he recovered enough to roar at the top of his lungs, "So this is how you value the outstanding work of a great Soviet artist, a master of Socialist Realism? Is this your attitude toward the Soviet Union? Is that what you want—another war?" Then he stormed into the office of the editor-in-chief.

I heard him shouting that he could not go on sharing space with a reactionary and demanding that something be done about it at once.

A great deal might have been done about it. The temper of the time did not allow for lack of enthusiasm, let alone criticism. That nothing was done was probably due to Rudolf's position and, in part, to the intelligence of the editor-in-chief who had replaced Stano and who was, despite twenty years in the Party, a rather sensible woman.

The anniversary of Victorious February was celebrated every year by a gala reception for several hundred guests at the Prague Castle and, in 1950, Rudolf and I were invited. The splendid halls were illuminated; all the historic treasures of the kings of Bohemia were on display. The refreshments were exquisite and a group of folk musicians in national costume provided the entertainment.

The short, very fat wife of the president, Marta Gottwald, resplendent in a kelly-green gown with a train, waddled between rows of obsequious bowing backs. The intellectuals among the guests seized the opportunity to besiege the buffet.

I was standing with a group of Rudolf's colleagues in one of the smaller salons when Klement Gottwald himself stumbled in on the arm of the Speaker of the National Assembly. The President of the Republic was sloshed; the Speaker was actually holding him up. Gottwald picked a path across the room straight toward me, lurched to a stop, and babbled, "What's the matter? You ain't drinking! Why ain't you drinking?"

The men around me signalled frantically for a waiter and, when one leaped forward with a tray, I took a glass of wine. So did the president. We both drank up. The president waved his empty glass in the air, stared at it for a moment, then fixed his bloodshot eyes on me and started babbling again, exactly as before, "What's the matter? You ain't drinking! Why ain't you drinking?"

The Speaker of the National Assembly was the first to regain his presence of mind. He laughed, managed to produce a few innocuous words, and started to maneuver the president out of the room. I stood there with the glass in my hand, feeling my knees shaking beneath the folds of my evening gown. That purple-red face, those dull, drunken eyes drowning in fat, that hoarse babble—this was our president! I spotted Rudolf in a far corner of the room and shot him a pleading look. We left soon after.

I spent the rest of the night sitting on the edge of the bathtub with a wet towel wrapped around my head. My ears were ringing with the rhythmic cheer of our Communist Youth Organization: *We are the future of our nation; we are Gottwald's generation!* And I remembered the tall, gracious figure of President Masaryk who had walked those magnificent Castle halls long ago, in the days of our innocence.

That episode badly jolted Rudolf as well. For some time it had been rumored that Gottwald drank, and that he had taken to drinking out of desperation over the Soviet failure to keep their word to let us run our country our own way. The president was ostensibly drowning in alcohol his pangs of conscience over the direction in which he had led his country. In February of 1948, much had been said about putting matters into the right hands. Now, two years later, it seemed as though matters had somehow slipped into the wrong ones.

By 1951, the atmosphere in Prague was almost as bad as it had been during the war. No one dared to speak out loud, and hardly a week passed without news of someone's arrest. The worst days were Thursday and Friday—my recollection is that the Central Committee met on Thursdays—and wherever a doorbell rang on those evenings, everyone turned pale. People who had not joined the Party now enjoyed a temporary respite; under the direct guidance of Soviet advisors whose task it was to purge the ranks, arrests made were mostly of Party members. There were a number of suicides, some quite mysterious, some entirely understandable. When one prominent official was told that two comrades in civilian clothes had come to visit and were waiting in his sitting room, he did not even bother to hear what they had to say. He took his revolver out of a drawer, left his house by the back door, and shot himself. It was later said that the two men had not come to arrest him but only to ask some questions. Or perhaps they had just dropped over for a glass of beer—who knows?

I was growing desperate. I wanted Rudolf to quit his job at any cost. I wanted to convince him that, if he stayed on, he could prevent nothing, improve nothing, that he could only destroy himself. "No person with any sense of self-respect," I argued, "can continue to be party to what's happening." But Rudolf, nervous and troubled, continued to stand his ground.

"On the contrary," he kept insisting. "If all the decent people leave now, things will get even worse."

I did not want to give up. I kept pleading with him, trying to prove my points, begging. We never quarrelled, but for months on end we did not exchange one personal remark, one intimate word. I knew I was making him suffer even more than he was already suffering and reproached myself for it. But I could not stop.

"What if they arrest you too?"

"That cannot happen," Rudolf would say. "Look, of course I don't believe that all the people who've been arrested have committed crimes. But it stands to reason that they must have made some serious mistakes. People cannot be held in jail for no reason at all. You have no idea how easy it is in this atmosphere to make a mistake, or to overlook something. And that can later be construed as intentional, as an act of sabotage. I'm sure that when the investigations are over and it's clear that there was no wrongdoing, they'll be released. It's tough, but that's the risk we took when we accepted our positions. Don't worry. My affairs are in perfect order. I'm so careful, no major mistake can slip by me."

"Rudolf, I beg you. . ."

"And I beg *you!* You're my wife. Show some confidence in me!"

Late in the spring of 1951, Rudolf became seriously ill. The doctor diagnosed his illness as complete nervous exhaustion and ordered rest. With that doctor's help, I finally managed to convince Rudolf to request permission to leave his job. I was so relieved when he agreed to do it that I even planned to give up my own job and drop my studies at the University. We would move out to the country. But my relief was short-lived. Rudolf's resignation was not accepted. He was merely granted a leave of absence for a few days and then everything returned to the way it was before.

One Saturday afternoon, Pavel Eisler came rushing into our apartment.

"Eda Goldstuecker has disappeared," he said. "Nobody knows where he is. Have you heard anything?"

Eduard Goldstuecker was one of Rudolf's and Pavel's oldest friends. He had returned a few days earlier from Israel, where he was serving as the Czechoslovak Ambassador. Relations between Israel and the Soviet Bloc had been deteriorating and we all knew that this had put Eda in an increasingly precarious position. But we had heard nothing about him and did not want to guess.

A few days later we found out that he, too, had been arrested. Rudolf did not say a word but, for several nights afterward, I would hear him pacing back and forth through the apartment, back and forth, while I lay in bed unable to sleep, staring helplessly into the darkness. Why do people's best intentions turn against them? Why hadn't we been able to foresee the consequences of our decisions?

"Rudolf," I asked timidly. "Doesn't it seem strange to you that so many of the people who are being arrested are Jews?"

Rudolf, usually so quiet, exploded. "For God's sake! Don't tell me you believe that the Communists are anti-Semites! How can you still not understand? You really should drop everything else you're doing and do some serious reading for a change!"

I believe it was in November of 1951 that the secretary general of the Party, Rudolf Slansky, was arrested. My husband had always intensely disliked Slansky. He considered him a dogmatic extremist, a vain and ruthless man, pathologically hungry for power and recognition. He had always avoided Slansky as much as possible and I knew that he had no official or personal connection with him. Slansky's contact in the Ministry of Foreign Trade was Rudolf's boss, the minister himself, so that my husband rarely had to encounter the almighty secretary general face to face.

When Slansky was arrested, we thought it meant a change was coming. It seemed logical since we assumed that the secretary general had been the one who had masterminded the reign of terror. But, in fact, just the opposite happened; the secret police, now known as State Security, intensified their rampage.

Late one Saturday night, I was sitting with Rudolf by lamplight in the window nook of our living room. It seemed to me that something of our former understanding was returning, something of our former confidence in each other. Our conversation was more relaxed. We managed to find words that held the same meaning for both of us. Our anxieties were now drawing us together just as our hopes had once done, and I dared to say what was on my mind without fear of hurting or angering him.

"I can't believe," I said, "that something inherently good can turn into its exact opposite just because of some mistakes or personal failures. If the system was fair and sound, it would provide ways of compensating for error. If it can only function when the leadership is made up of geniuses and all the people are one hundred percent honest and infallible, then it's a bad system. It might work in heaven but it's a foolish and destructive illusion for this world. Look at all those idealists who wanted nothing more than to work for the well-being of others; half of them are in jail; the other half start trembling every time their doorbell rings. It's all one big fraud—a trap for naive, trusting fools."

Rudolf got up and paced the room a few times. Then he stood by the window with his back to me, opened the curtains and looked out into the darkness for a while.

"Heda," he said, "you know how much my work means to me. I've given it all that's good in me. And it's not only that. I thought that with this job, life had offered me a chance to do some good, to make up for our passivity in the past. I know I've been a bad husband and a bad father for the last two years. I've neglected you for the sake of my work. I've denied myself everything I love. But there is one thing I cannot give up: I cannot give up my conviction that my ideal is essentially sound and good, just as I cannot explain why it has failed—as it apparently has. I still believe this is a crisis that will pass. If you're right, if it really is a fraud, then I've been an accomplice in a terrible crime. And if I had to believe that, I could not go on living . . . I would not want to. . . . "

That was our last conversation on the subject. The year 1951 was drawing to its close.

One evening, during the first week of 1952, we left home to attend yet another official reception. All these affairs have long since merged into one and I no longer remember where it was held. As we got into the car, I said to Rudolf, "Look at that man standing on the corner. I've seen him there every time I've left the house the past few days."

Rudolf laughed.

"He probably likes some girl who works in the store across the street. What's the matter with you? You need a rest. Ask for a vacation and take the boy to the mountains."

At that reception, I remember receiving the special attentions of Comrade Minister Siroky, the head of the cabinet. He took my arm, pressed the palm of his hand against mine, and strolled around with me for a long while—something he had never done before. Comrade Morozov from the Soviet Trade Mission was also especially cordial. As usual, the vodka was running in streams, and toasts were made to the health of a large number of people who would have served humanity best by not having been born.

On the tenth of January, after work, I stopped at the bank to get some cash. I wanted to buy fabric for a suit for Rudolf. But when I got to the fabric store, it was so crowded with people fighting over bolts of material and there was so long a line at the cashier's desk that I walked out in disgust. The same scene was being played out in most of the stores in Prague. The city once again looked like an anthill that someone had stirred up with a stick. People were rushing nervously through the streets and forming long lines on the sidewalks in front of every store.

It was clear that a rumor of another currency devaluation had spread through the grapevine again. Sometimes these rumors were instigated by the Ministry of Domestic Trade when warehouses began to pile up too much defective merchandise that no one wanted to buy. A hint here and there that a currency reform was being contemplated would suffice to send people out into the streets buying up anything they could lay their hands on before their savings were either devalued or entirely lost.

I caught a streetcar home where Mrs. Machova was playing with my son. Ivan was already attending nursery school by then. He took after his father in almost every way. He was a quiet, serious child, intelligent and happy. He seemed entirely unaffected by the atmosphere of our home which, at the time, was not exactly cheerful.

After dinner, when we had put Ivan to bed, Mrs. Machova and I began to grumble about the situation in the stores and were going strong when Rudolf came home. We attacked him together. This is intolerable so many years after the war! It's almost worse than under the Occupation! How much longer can it go on?

"It's all because people have given up expecting anything good from this government," said Mrs. Machova. "Our government has no intention of taking care of us. It only harrasses us. Whenever the Central Committee meets or the government is in session, people just shudder and wonder what kind of shabby deal they'll come up with next."

Mrs. Machova was one of those people on whose behalf the Party had made the revolution. She was the daughter of a poor peasant, the wife of a blue collar worker, who herself had worked hard all her life. She had had only an elementary school education but she was perhaps the wisest, most astute woman I had ever met. Rudolf, too, had endless respect for her. Her voice, he understood, was the authentic voice of the working class which everybody talked about but to which no one actually listened.

Wearily and unhappily, Rudolf tried to pacify us but, by then, my last reserves of patience were gone. After Mrs. Machova left, he tried to take me in his arms for a reconciliation and a good night kiss. I turned my head and pushed him away. For the first time in our life together we went to sleep without making up, without a word.

We did not speak to each other the next morning either but that was not unusual; I started work at seven, Rudolf got up one hour later. All day long, I felt unhappy about my unkindness and my stubborness the night before, and I resolved to set things right. The constant tension and fear had so exhausted and transformed me that I could barely recognize myself. This can't go on, I decided. I must get a better grip on things or else there won't be any living with me. I have to stop being afraid. I have to get rid of these premonitions. I've survived worse without turning into a repulsive shrew. I will simply not give in to my moods anymore.

That afternoon, I took my son for a long walk. I bought fresh flowers for the house—florists were the only shops that had no lines before them—and that evening I started planning my new life. I would exercise every day, beginning today. I would see my friends more frequently; I would be sure to go to the theater and to concerts more often; I would spend more time with my son.

I called Rudolf at the office and asked what time he would be home. He told me that he still had piles of work on his desk but that he would try to hurry. I put Dvořak's Humoresque on the phonograph together with some other records and took our copy of *The Good Soldier Schweik* from the bookcase. Tonight, I thought, I'll have a quiet pleasant evening.

I called Rudolf again at ten o'clock.

"I haven't finished yet," he said. "It'll probably be another late night. Go to sleep. I'll come home as soon as I can."

I went into the bathroom, did half an hour of honest exercise, spent another quarter of an hour in a hot bath, and tried to talk myself into feeling light-hearted and gay. Everything always depends on the attitude one brings to things. From now on, I'll look at all of our problems with a cool detachment.

But I could not fall asleep. Shortly before midnight, I got up and took two tablets of aspirin. At one o'clock, the doorbell rang.

Marenka, the young woman who had been living with us since I had returned to work and who helped take care of Ivan as well as the household, burst into my bedroom and stammered, "There are five men at the door and they have Dr. Margolius' briefcase!"

The world tilted and I felt myself falling, bound hand and foot, down, farther down, tumbling ever faster into a bottomless space. And then I snapped awake. So here it is. I knew it had to come and here it is. Here it is again.

It was a strange moment. I found myself accepting horror and disaster as though an old companion who had taken leave of me for a while was now back beside me. And then another familiar sensation took hold of me—that inner bracing of strength we discover when the worst has happened, when we know there is no way out and there can be no help coming from anyone but ourselves. It springs from a source so deeply hidden that we are unaware it exists, but it always comes to the rescue when life bares its fangs and attacks.

I got out of bed, put on my slippers, and combed my hair. The only unusual thing I did was to put on Rudolf's robe instead of my own. It reached all the way down to my ankles, covering me completely.

I went out into the living room and, sure enough, there were five men standing there, one of them holding Rudolf's briefcase. They greeted me with exaggerated courtesy, announced that my husband had been arrested, and that they had been authorized to carry out a search of the house. I told them to go ahead and then turned around intending to go back into the bedroom, but they stopped me and explained, again very politely, that the law required my presence during the search to ensure that everything had been done in an orderly way.

So I sat down in a chair, lit a cigarette, and watched the comrades get to work. Their search was thorough. They moved systematically from room to room, opening drawers and closets, examining every one of several hundred books, unfolding and reading every scrap of paper. They looked under the rugs and among the dishes. They searched every piece of clothing in our closets, fingering the seams. They inspected our shoes and toiletries. They set aside a few things—foreign-language publications evoked their greatest interest.

A few days earlier, someone had brought us several packages of Albanian cigarettes. Each one contained a little leaflet with an inscription in Albanian. Because the group of words ended with an exclamation point it probably was some slogan like "Long live the working class!" but my visitors collected the leaflets carefully and added them to their pile.

The man who appeared to be in charge read all my private correspondence, uttered a few appreciative remarks as to the literary quality of the letters, and confiscated one or two of them. He paid particular attention to my diary, which was a few years old and in which I had kept a record of my son's measurements and weight. Those numbers evidently impressed him as some ingenious code; when he put the diary onto his pile, he gave me a particularly devastating look. I remained seated in my chair wearing Rudolf's robe, trying not to smoke one cigarette after another.

I only spoke up when they started for the nursery. What if the boy wakes up and sees five strange men rummaging through his toys? Who knows what consequences such a shock could have? I gave them my word of honor that the room contained nothing but Ivan's things. They insisted that they had to search the whole apartment but promised to be as quiet as possible. They kept that promise and searched the room so expertly that Ivan never once woke up.

Marenka's room was next. She had gone back to bed after waking me. Now one of the men opened the door to her room and she got up, protesting. When he began rummaging through her possessions she showered him with such biting comments that he emerged blushing bright red. I have often since felt grateful to Marenka for her performance, but of course as a member of the exploited proletariat she could get away with it.

They saved for last the room that contained my desk, and in it our most important documents and valuables. They included a special file of my correspondence with friends who now lived abroad, especially in England. It was Rudolf's wish that I keep all their letters as well as carbon copies of my replies in a separate file so as to be able to prove, if ever necessary, that they contained no objectionable material.

But now everything would be considered objectionable. The simplest sentence could be construed as a secret code and the mere fact that I had kept regularly in touch with the West would certainly be turned into damaging evidence against Rudolf. I waited dejectedly for the glee with which they would pounce on this booty. The man who opened the compartment in which the file was kept was the only one who had been openly hostile to me throughout the proceedings. The four others had been ostentatiously polite, but this fifth man kept glaring at me and dropping such rude, insulting remarks that finally the leader of the group rebuked him. My heart sank as this ferret took the dangerous file into his hands. I braced myself. He opened it without batting an eyelash, closed it immediately, and pushed it far back into the compartment, behind some odds and ends. I could not believe my eyes.

Meanwhile the man in charge was digging through the drawer which contained our cash and two savings account passbooks. He announced that he was obliged to confiscate all of it but set aside one bill which he left in the drawer. It was a note for one thousand crowns, then worth about twenty dollars. I pointed out that the cash he was confiscating included my previous month's salary and that both savings accounts were in my name. He replied politely that he was only following orders; I had the right to request the return of my personal property at a later time.

He took all of Rudolf's documents, his camera, his car keys, his garage key, and various other small things. Then he turned to look for my handbag, but before he could reach it, the boor snatched it up with another snide remark, carted it off to the light of the lamp, and opened it. I remembered the ten thousand-crown bills that I had withdrawn from the bank for Rudolf's suit. They were still in my handbag, in an open envelope. The man busied himself with my things for quite a while. He inspected my compact and my change purse, muttered some more unpleasant things, pulled out my brand-new calendar which as yet had nothing written in it, and threw it on top of the pile of confiscated items. Then he snapped the handbag shut and dropped it on a table.

By that time it was nearly six in the morning. One of the men wrote up a report for me to sign and then, finally, they left.

I wandered from room to room for a while, trying to gather my thoughts. Poor Marenka sniffled in the kitchen over a pot of coffee. I don't think she liked me very much, but she adored Rudolf.

I have to pull myself together, I thought. I have to be calm and self-confident so that it is clear to everyone that I am absolutely certain of Rudolf's innocence. I must not think of how he must be feeling or what they might be doing to him. I have to concentrate on finding the best way to help him. First, I go to the office and tell them what has happened. Then I go see every influential acquaintance we have.

Only then did I realize how few influential people I knew well enough to ask for help. First of all, I decided, I would call Rudolf's boss, Minister of Foreign Trade Antonin Gregor. After all, Rudolf was his immediate subordinate, his deputy minister. He could not have done anything without Gregor's authorization. Gregor was routinely informed of every move Rudolf made—he had to stand by him. And the other deputy minister, Jonas, had always treated us like close friends, if not relations. He would hug me whenever we met. I would call both of them as soon as their offices opened. I threw off Rudolf's robe, dressed, and forced a cup of Marenka's black coffee down my throat. Before I left, I went into the nursery to check on Ivan. He was fast asleep, smiling, his cheeks flushed. Nothing had touched him yet.

At that time my editor-in-chief was Jura Zajonc, a bright, good-natured young man who came from a long line of miners. He was, of course, a dedicated Communist, but I had always suspected he had a mind of his own. Walking into his office with my news was not exactly easy, but I thought it lucky to be delivering it to him.

Jura listened to what I had to say in silence, pondered it, then said, "We have to hope that this thing will somehow be resolved.

I don't know your husband but I do know you. For the moment, I see no reason why you shouldn't stay here and go on with your work."

"Do I have to let the whole office know?"

"I wouldn't say anything to anyone yet. What if your husband comes back home in a few days?"

Had I been able to smile that day, it would have been at that moment. If Jura thought it possible that Rudolf could come home, why couldn't it happen? Maybe they would discover that they had arrested a totally innocent man. And Rudolf had been so confident that he had overlooked nothing, that he had made no mistakes.

I went into my studio and dialed my first number.

"May I speak with Comrade Minister Gregor?"

"Who's calling?"

"Mrs. Margolius."

"The Comrade Minister is not in."

I dialed the second number.

"May I speak with Comrade Deputy Minister Jonas?"

"Who's calling?"

"Mrs. Margolius."

"The Comrade Deputy is not in."

Maybe it was true. Maybe they were both in meetings. I would call back later in the morning. Meanwhile I would go to see Deputy Minister of Foreign Affairs Vlastimil Borek. He was a distant relative of Rudolf's and very fond of him. Borek was an older man, a highly respected prewar Party member and a former newspaperman who knew everyone who mattered. Later that year, during the trials, he would behave badly, testifying against his colleagues at the Ministry. Soon afterward he would die under rather mysterious circumstances; his own wife could not be sure whether or not his was a natural death.

I called Borek and could tell from the tone of his voice that he had not yet been informed. I asked whether I could see him right away and, surprised, he said, "Come on over."

When I told him about Rudolf's arrest, Borek turned pale. He tried to pull himself together, but for a few moments, all he could

112

do was repeat, "So he too . . . he, too . . ." I was not sure what he meant by that. We talked, and I begged him to use his influence on Rudolf's behalf. He promised solemnly to do all he could.

I hurried back to my office. I must not give them any reason to fire me, I thought. I must work harder and better than ever. I stayed in my studio that entire afternoon. I knew how worn out I looked and I wanted to avoid any questions. Every hour I stopped my work to call the Ministry, but none of Rudolf's colleagues were in, and finally I had to admit that this was no coincidence. None of them would speak with me. Even if I somehow should manage to reach them, they would do nothing. They were all terrified and trying their best to avoid showing any semblance of sympathy for Rudolf. None would lift a finger for him.

After work I stopped at a telephone booth and called Pavel Eisler. He was the best and staunchest friend I had and a man of great political insight. He was an economist by training, who had worked at the United Nations under Gunnar Myrdal after the war. When he had returned to Prague, his connections had at first been greatly appreciated; a few years later, they had become dangerous liabilities. Now he was performing unskilled labor in a factory, earning next to nothing and anticipating arrest at any moment. No one understood how it had happened that he remained free for so long. The only possible explanation was that his wife was the daughter of Lord Layton, an influential Englishman and a personal friend of Winston Churchill—clearly someone who could cause a great deal of trouble were his son-in-law to be arrested.

Even so, I knew Pavel's situation was precarious and I did not wish to make it worse by drawing attention to his friendship with Rudolf. When he answered the phone I tried to disguise my voice. "Pavel, my husband went to see Eda," I said softly. "I feel lonely. I'd like to talk but don't know if you have the time."

There was a moment of shocked silence and then Pavel shouted, "Heda, you fool! Of course we have to talk! Come over right away!"

"I'd rather come in the evening."

"Fine! Come in the evening."

I went home. Mrs. Machova, whose infallible instinct led her to turn up at our house when we most needed her, was in the kitchen talking with Marenka. I could see that both of them had been weeping.

It was then I learned that Rudolf's arrest had been staged like the climactic scene of a spy thriller. The whole street had been lit up by the headlights of black police cars positioned at strategic angles and manned by members of State Security. When Rudolf's car had turned the corner, the police had blocked off all possible escape routes and, as he got out, several agents had surrounded him, had disarmed him by seizing his briefcase, and had pronounced him under arrest. This intrepid maneuver on the part of the secret police had awed the inhabitants of the entire neighborhood.

My son was busy playing with his toy train in the living room. I sat beside him on the floor and watched him. Then, as casually as I could, I told him that his father had gone away on yet another one of his business trips. Ivan was used to that. He just nodded and then let out a screech as his train took a sharp curve. He was fully absorbed in his world.

I put him to bed as early as I could and set out to see the Eislers. When I reached the streetcar stop, it occurred to me that I, too, probably had the secret police on my back. I looked around the traffic island. A few people were standing there but no one seemed to be paying particular attention to me. The streetcar came. I stood still while almost everyone else got on. Only when the car began to move did I jump aboard. Out of the corner of my eye I saw that a young man who had been leaning against a lamp post reading a newspaper jumped on at the other end of the car.

Aha! I got off at the next stop. So did he. He went into a telephone booth. I got into another streetcar, headed away from the Eislers' home, and he remained in the booth. At the next stop, I took a third car going in the opposite direction from the second and continued to switch until I decided that, if I had not eluded my pursuers, I had at least given them a run for their money. None of this mattered anyway, I thought, if State Security was keeping

Pavel's house under surveillance which, I later discovered, was the case. They kept a record of everyone who visited him and, because the Eislers were always willing to listen—they could not help; no one could—and give advice to the many wives and children of men who had been arrested, the agents nicknamed Pavel "the patron saint of widows and orphans."

I sat there long into the night, discussing what to do. Pavel's advice was: do everything and expect nothing. Do not leave any stone unturned. See everyone you can think of. Write. Call. Do not allow them to silence you. If they do not return your calls, call again the next day. If they do not answer your letters, write again. Pester them like a guilty conscience. But be careful when you cross the street so that you don't happen to get run over by one of their nicely-polished black limousines.

Pavel helped me draft a letter to President Gottwald and to the Central Committee. I was afraid that, with my lack of political finesse, I might write something that would exacerbate Rudolf's situation instead of improving it. We also agreed that I had to find a lawyer who would not be afraid of taking on Rudolf's case.

Then Pavel asked me, "Did you keep an eye on those men all the time they were in your apartment?"

"I think so. Why?"

"I wouldn't be surprised if they had bugged it."

"I don't think they could have," I began. "They didn't have any opportunity to . . ." And then I remembered an episode that had taken place when Rudolf had been appointed Deputy Minister that had appeared trivial at the time. A "hot line" that connected our home to various offices had been installed in addition to our regular telephone. As the nice, elderly telephone man was leaving, he had said, "You know, I wouldn't want a phone like this in my place for all the money in the world!"

I had just laughed when he said that and had not given the matter a second thought. Now it dawned on me that the man had probably wanted to warn me that the telephone he had put in was bugged. And this was the telephone we kept in our bedroom, the room that was separated from the rest of the apartment, to which

115

I liked to retreat with friends whenever we wished to talk freely! The regime had spied on us right from the start, from the moment it had entrusted Rudolf with an important official position.

Late that night, when I finally got to bed, I allowed myself for the first time to think of Rudolf—what he might be feeling and thinking, what they might be doing to him. I lay there without moving, and the darkness pierced my heart like a black spike. I could at least hope that people were no longer subjected to torture during interrogations as they had been under the Nazis, that they were treated with minimal decency. But even if that were true, how terrible Rudolf must feel! I kept hearing him say, "I could not go on living . . . I would not want to." No. He had to hold on, he could not give up. Maybe they would only question him and then let him go. Such things had been known to have happened. I heard the elevator start up in the hall below and my heart jumped. He was coming! Now the elevator would stop at our floor. I would hear his key in the lock, and the door would open. . . . But the elevator passed by our floor without stopping.

The following afternoon I was sitting in the office of the chairman of the Economic Commission of the Party, Ludvik Frejka. I knew him only slightly, but he had always seemed a kind man and vaguely reminded me of one of my uncles. In fact, he now received me as an older relative might, hunching despondently behind his huge desk. He had already heard about Rudolf's arrest, and I had the feeling that he knew much more, none of it good. He sighed and said, "My dear girl, you have no idea how much I appreciate Rudolf and how much I would like to help both of you. Only a year ago, I might have been able to pull a few strings. Then I was still a deserving old Communist. Today they think of me only as a dirty Jew. I'm in no position to help you. I can't even help myself."

A few weeks later, he, too, was arrested.

It was the same story with Pavel Kavan, Rudolf's friend at the Ministry of Foreign Affairs. He was fired shortly after I saw him and arrested a few months later.

The only other official who agreed to see me was Bohumil

Sucharda, then a deputy minister of finance. I knew he could do nothing for Rudolf but I was grateful to him for receiving me courageously in his office and for speaking of my husband with confidence and trust.

Other doors remained firmly closed. Of all the high-ranking comrades who were my husband's colleagues, the only one to pay me a visit was Ota Klicka, our Ambassador to Finland. One day he appeared at the door of our apartment, unexpectedly, and said, "I've known Rudolf since we went to school together and I will never believe he did anything dishonest. I'd stake my life on it. All this is utter nonsense!"

By that time, I had become like a leper, to be avoided by anyone who valued his life. Even the most casual encounter with me could arouse suspicion and invite disaster. I understood that and could bear the isolation better than most people in the same situation. The war had inured me to it and, besides, I knew that I had no right to expose other people to danger. Why should anyone risk his job or the safety of his family or, perhaps, his freedom, just to talk to me? It is natural for people to think first of those for whom they are responsible. If everyone were a hero, what would courage be worth? And so it was largely without bitterness that I watched people suddenly cross the street when they saw me coming or, if they spotted me too late to cross, avert their eyes. To those few who insisted on continuing their acquaintance with me, I myself would say, "Don't stop. Don't talk to me. It makes no sense."

Several good friends, all people I had known for years, stood by me. They believed in Rudolf and it did not occur to them to condemn him, although none were Party members and none had ever agreed with his political views. Almost all of them had already lost their jobs and were living from one day to the next. So far, the parents of the children living in our building still allowed my child to play with theirs, so that he, at least, did not suffer from loneliness. State Security kept tabs on everyone I had met, and as a result some of these people—such as the family of the publisher for whom I had worked before the coup—were ruthlessly interrogated. Not to turn away from me required enormous courage.

One afternoon a few months after Rudolf's arrest, I was coming home from work and passed the house where Dr. Padovcova lived. She was a pediatrician who had taken care of my child from the time of his birth and who had become a friend. She was well-known for helping all kinds of outcasts. That day I felt such an overwhelming loneliness that I decided to visit with her for a few minutes even though I had never done anything as imprudent before. I took the elevator up to her floor and rang her bell. My friend opened the door, her face white. "No we don't have the keys to the laundry room," she said loudly. "Ask the people next door!"

"Okay, okay," I yelled in the coarsest voice I could muster and I turned around and ran down the stairs.

I found out later that State Security had arrived at her apartment just a few minutes ahead of me, barging in on my friend and Magda Husakova, the wife of Gustav Husak who was to become President of the Republic after the Russian Occupation in 1968. But, at the time, he too was in jail. Had the secret police found me there as well, they would certainly have concluded that we were conspiring against the state, and would have arrested all three of us. As it was, they only turned the apartment upside down and left. This was everyday life in Czechoslovakia in 1952.

When Pavel Kavan was arrested, I became close to his wife Rosemary, an Englishwoman who had two children about the same age as my son. She and I joined forces and would help each other out for years to come, often sharing our last ten-crown note or a bit of food for the children. Rosemary died a few years ago, but I can still see the look of concentration on her face as she tried to cut one hard-boiled egg into three equal parts: one piece for each child. The only bright side of our life at that time was that it forged such extraordinary human relationships, friendships of a kind that are rarely possible among free, untroubled people.

A few days after Rudolf's arrest, I found a lawyer who was said to have excellent connections at the highest level and who handled political cases. Dr. Bartos received me very formally, addressed me not as "Comrade" but as "My dear Mrs. Margolius," in the old bourgeois style, and promised to defend Rudolf.

118

We both knew, of course, that the legal practice of the time effectively prevented a counsel for the defense from doing much for his client. The presence of an attorney at a trial was sheer formality, the accused having been found guilty even before he stepped into the courtroom. Still, I wanted Rudolf to have the benefit of legal advice, whatever it was worth.

I told Dr. Bartos that, at the moment, I was penniless but that State Security had confiscated our savings accounts which contained money I had inherited from my mother. Should he succeed in having them returned to me, I would be able to pay him for his services.

About two weeks after his arrest, I received my first short letter from Rudolf. No matter how often I reread it, I could not discover anything more in it than the information that he was well and that he did not want me to worry.

At that point, I was still not over my initial shock. I was still trying not to think, not to despair, trying to carry out all my duties at home and at work like a machine. Office in the morning. Useless attempts at talks with influential officials in the afternoon. In the evenings thinking up, then writing innumerable letters in which I swore that my husband was innocent, offered testimony of my own and that of his friends on his behalf, argued, pleaded, sometimes almost threatened. During the nights, which were worse than the days, I would lie in bed for hours unable to sleep, saying aloud into the deaf darkness, "Rudolf, hold on. Please, hold on. Resist."

My position at the publishing house became more and more unpleasant. No one spoke an unnecessary word to me. Conversations stopped and faces froze whenever I entered a room. These embarrassments, however, did not last very long. About a month after Rudolf's arrest, my editor-in-chief called me into his office and, gently, explained that he had received instructions "from above" to fire me.

I had, of course, been expecting to lose my job for some time but, until it happened, I had refused to worry about it. I knew that if I was to keep my sanity, I had to resolve problems as they came up, one by one, that I had to force myself to think no more than one day ahead. But now there could be no more stalling.

119

The loss of my job meant not only being unable to support myself and my child. It also provided the police with an excuse to arrest me as a "parasite," an individual who refused to contribute to the building of socialist society. In Czechoslovakia, as in all the Communist countries of Europe at the time, being unemployed was not merely unfortunate; it was illegal. But in a country where all jobs had become government jobs, who would employ an outcast like myself?

I lived a few days of utter horror before help arrived, again through friends. Otto and Milena had managed to persuade the manager of a machine shop which already employed several people with questionable political profiles to give me a job. The wages were minuscule; they did not even suffice to pay my rent. But, at least, I was not unemployed.

That evening, I sat down for a conference with Marenka. I told her that I would no longer be able to pay her wages. She was, however, welcome to continue living in the apartment and I would try to provide food for all three of us. In return, I asked her to help me take care of Ivan. My new job demanded that I alternate work shifts: one week, I would work from six in the morning until two in the afternoon; the next, from two in the afternoon until ten at night. I asked Marenka to take my son to his nursery school when I worked the morning shift; to pick him up, feed him supper, and put him to bed when I worked at night.

Marenka agreed. A few days later, she found a good job in a bakery which she liked very much and, often when things were the most difficult, she would bring Ivan a roll or a few cookies. She arranged her shifts to complement mine so that the child was never alone.

The months that followed were like a merry-go-round gone berserk. I have an innate incompetence for anything mechanical. It has always seemed to me that a machine can tell from far away that I am afraid of it and that I don't understand anything about it, and breaks down on the spot out of sheer self-preservation. In my new job, my relationship with machines took on the dimensions of a primordial conflict. I tried desperately just to reach a level of average productivity but never could, and no other machine broke down as often as mine. There was a productivity ladder which hung on the wall of our shop, on which all the workers were ranked in order of proficiency. My place was always second from the bottom. The last rung belonged permanently to a chubby blonde whose intellectual development seemed somewhat retarded. I often stayed at work long after everyone else had left in order to make up for what I had been unable to produce during working hours, but even so my output did not improve. Moreover, the deafening noise of the machines combined with my constant tension began to cause me unbearable headaches, which throbbed on for hours after I went home.

My financial situation was an even bigger headache. I had to feed three people, pay an outrageous rent, and, most importantly, send a little money to Rudolf each month, not only to enable him to supplement his rations and buy cigarettes or other things, but to show him that we were all right, that he should not worry. I had to find some way of getting rid of my exorbitant rent, so I looked around until I found an inexpensive, small apartment whose occupants were eager to swap flats with me. I was getting ready to move, when I was officially notified that, in order to leave my old apartment, I would need written permission from the Ministry of Foreign Trade. I applied and, in answer to my application, the Ministry informed me that our apartment belonged not to Rudolf or me but to the Ministry itself. I could not move out until my husband's case was "resolved."

I replied heatedly that I could not understand how an apartment that I myself had found and for which I had been paying rent could possibly belong to the Ministry and again requested permission to move. The correspondence dragged on for a year unresolved. Ours was a desirable apartment in a desirable neighborhood. As there was a critical shortage of any kind of housing at all, the comrades at the Ministry were determined to hang on to it. If I moved, the apartment would no longer be under their control. If they managed to keep me there until my husband was convicted, they could throw me out into the street and the place would be theirs.

There was no alternative but to find another source of income.

Fortunately, at first, I managed to find enough work to keep my head above water. Using assumed names, I drew illustrations for children's magazines and copied technical drawings. I did whatever work I could find. I worked my eight-hour shift at the machine and then at least six hours more at home. Often I walked back and forth from the shop in order to save the money I would have paid for the tram. At night I kept writing my stubborn missives to the ministries, to the Central Committee, to the President, to the Office of the Prime Minister, to any influential person I could think of.

I never received any replies—except one from the Office of the President which informed me, drily, that my husband's case would be "investigated."

Sometimes I slept only three or four hours a night, but I made it an iron rule never to work on Sunday afternoons and to make sure to save up enough money so that every week Ivan and I could take the streetcar to the outskirts of Prague and walk in the woods. In spring, we played in the grass and sailed little boats in the brook in the wooded valley just beyond the last stop of the streetcar.

Night after night, I dreamed the same dream. I would be sitting in some public place—a restaurant or cafe or concert hall. Suddenly a door would open, Rudolf would come in, and then stop. I would sit in my chair as if I were nailed to it and could not move. He would stand there looking at me, never coming even one step closer.

Once a month, I received a letter from Rudolf and, once a month, I was allowed to send him a reply. Those letters had to be strictly personal of course. Not a word about where he was or what was happening to him. We both knew that as much as one careless reference might prevent the letter from being delivered. From what Rudolf wrote, I could see that he had decided to focus completely on the past. He wrote a great deal about his son and I could see how much he regretted not having spent more time with him. His letters revived hundreds of moments that I had already forgotten.

"Do you remember," he wrote, "how we first met?"

122

It had been a beautiful spring day. I was about twelve years old and ran across the street to buy a bag of marbles. A young man wearing glasses was walking in the street toward me. He looked at me intently and smiled.

It seemed odd to me that a grown-up man was paying me such attention and, still running, I looked back at him over my shoulder. He was standing in the street, watching me.

That evening, Rudolf went out with a group of his friends, which included my older cousin who was much taken with him at the time. While they were dancing, Rudolf told her, "I met a little girl today whom I'm going to wait for. When she grows up, I'll marry her."

Some time later we met again—at a tea party given by that same cousin. As soon as I walked in, Rudolf came to my side and, from that moment on, became my great friend. He helped me when I had trouble with my homework and put in a good word for me with my parents when I misbehaved; he took me to lectures and to the theater and waited patiently for me to grow up. Our relationship had the strength of a love that grows out of trust and long understanding. In spite of everything that had separated us, we always knew that we belonged together and that it could never be any other way.

It was a great comfort to me that Rudolf was able to find happy memories in our difficult past and that these memories were helping him survive. Several times he wrote about our spring in the woods, so clear and cool, to which we used to walk and then sit motionless for hours, waiting for the young deer to come and drink. Years later I went back to that village and looked for our spring, but there was nothing left. All I found was a hollow among the tree roots, full of dry leaves.

In the letters I wrote to Rudolf, I described our everyday life as cheerfully as I could. Every night, I made notes of the day's events so that I was sure not to leave out anything of interest, and I tried hard to give him the impression that we were doing well. In each letter, I mentioned some event, mostly taken from our experience during the war, that had required strength of will, self-confidence, and courage. I think he understood what I was trying to tell him—that those qualities would help him now as they had then, and that just as I had stood by him always, I was with him now.

We both lied in those letters. We lied in all the things we did not say. But, in those things we did say, we revealed to each other the only truth that matters.

I never sent my letters by mail. I delivered each one of them myself to a special department at Police Headquarters in Bartolomejska Street. I still do not know what I expected from those very unpleasant visits but I told myself then that they gave me an opportunity to reach at least the most superficial layer of the power structure. Maybe I would be able to find out something. Maybe I would meet someone able and willing to make Rudolf's ordeal a little easier. Each time I came to deliver a letter at Headquarters, I had to pass several checkpoints guarded by uniformed police, who questioned me at length. Most of them were women who rarely missed an opportunity to insult and humiliate me, so that entering that building came to feel like descending into a lion's den. I had an arrangement with Mrs. Machova that I would call as soon as I left the building. If ever I did not call, she was to hurry to my apartment and get Ivan out. From the start, I had worked out a detailed plan to prevent my son from falling into the hands of the police were I ever arrested. When both parents of a child were jailed, the child was placed in an institution, subjected to every kind of hardship, and taught hate and contempt for his parents.

The security agent who took my letters always treated me with an appropriate degree of rudeness, but after a while we established an odd relationship that reminded me of the stories from the first world war, about soldiers in opposing trenches who called out to each other just like ordinary people in those moments when the firing stopped, only to pick up their rifles a few minutes later and shoot at one another. I think that security agent found my perseverance amusing. From his comments I concluded, probably wrongly, that he saw Rudolf personally, and eventually I came to regard him as an intermediary, a connecting link between us.

I had been trying for some time to find a way to help Rudolf. I was convinced that there had to be a crack somewhere in the monolith of State Security—it was just a matter of finding it. Then, late one evening, an older woman wearing a kerchief appeared at my door and, after making sure we were alone, said, "You don't know who I am and I won't tell you that or who has sent me. I have just come to warn you not to try anything. You can only do harm. There is a man who knows your husband well and knows he is innocent. He has inside information about the case and wants to help. But for the time being, nothing can be done. He asked me to tell you this: Your husband's file is marked with the letter S."

That was all. The woman left without another word.

The letter S? What did that mean? I racked my brains in vain. The next day, right after work, I dropped everything and ran to see the Eislers. Pavel knew a thousand times more about Rudolf's activities than I did. Maybe he could figure it out. But he could not.

We pondered it for weeks, guessed and speculated, sifted through all of Rudolf's actions, acquaintances, and contacts, even the most unlikely possibilities.

Not one of us imagined that the mysterious "S" stood for "Slansky Case."

Life in Prague, from which I was almost entirely excluded by this time, had acquired a totally negative character. People no longer aspired toward things but away from them. All they wanted was to avoid trouble. They tried not to be seen anywhere, not to talk to anyone, not to attract any attention. Their greatest satisfaction would be that nothing happened, that no one had been fired or arrested or questioned or followed by the secret police. Some fifty thousand people had so far been jailed in our small country. More were disappearing every day.

I still had no idea where Rudolf was being held. In one letter he mentioned that sometimes, at night, he could hear a nightingale sing and, from this, I deduced that he was not being held in Prague. But it took me a long time to find out about the prison in Ruzyn, which deserves to be ranked alongside the most notorious Nazi torture chambers.

Next to my suffocating fear for Rudolf and for the future of my child, I was most troubled by the impossibility of earning a living. No matter how hard or how long I worked, I could not manage to make enough money to cover our basic needs. My landlady developed a habit of coming into our apartment when we were away and carting off anything of value, just in case I would not be able to pay her murderous rent. These periodic raids so enraged me that I began to sell off my possessions myself, rashly, at ridiculous prices. I was sick with worry, and maybe the reason why my machine worked so poorly was that it was rusting inside from all the tears that had rolled into it.

From time to time, my son would ask when his father was coming back home, and I always managed to come up with some convincing answer. I read him the parts of Rudolf's letters that his father had written especially for him and, whenever he wondered why his father wrote home so infrequently, I would write out a letter from him myself.

Summer came. Ivan, who was pale, skinny, and tense despite all my efforts, badly needed some country air. Rudolf had one relative who had survived the war, his cousin Marie, who lived in Bratislava. Her husband had been thrown out of work because of his connection with Rudolf and was now supporting five people on a tiny income. I knew how difficult their life was and did not want to ask them for help, but one day I received an unexpected letter from Marie herself saying that she was taking her children to the country to visit their grandmother and that she would like to take my son along with them. This was a stroke of luck I had not dared dream of. I promised to send along as much money as I could and sent Ivan off to fresh air.

As soon as my son left, I redoubled my efforts to find additional work, but it was becoming increasingly hard to find. By now I had become more dangerous than the plague and fear—the fear of people who lived or worked around me—locked me into an ever stricter quarantine.

During this time, I was notified that Rudolf had been expelled from the Party. That was a bad sign; evidently his interrogation had taken a turn for the worse. Because his ouster was announced in the local Party organization, my own situation worsened as well. Until then, the people on our street had simply ignored or avoided me; now a wave of hatred began to swell. Women particularly would stop and stare at me with venom, whispering among themselves as I walked by. Sometimes a comrade concierge would spit onto the sidewalk after I passed her door, loudly, making sure I noticed. I felt thankful that my son was away in the country. While he was gone, moreover, I saved money by living on bread and milk which I bought at stores I passed on my way home from work. Entering stores in my own neighborhood had become a severe test in self-control.

Prague was sweltering with midsummer heat and my isolation was complete. My friends had left for their vacations, my child and Marenka were both away, and my one-sided nocturnal conversations with Rudolf had become stifled by fatigue and despair.

One afternoon, the doorbell that had been silent for weeks suddenly rang. Two people stood at the door, a man and a woman. They introduced themselves as inspectors from the local National Committee who had come to secure the property of Dr. Rudolf Margolius. Stunned, I let them in. Confiscation of property? Surely that was not done until after the conviction! Had Rudolf been tried already without my knowing about it? What was the verdict? What had they done with him? Where was he? Then the room went dark, the red carpet swung up toward me and hit me on the head.

I came to in a puddle of cold water with two grotesquely distorted faces floating above me. My two visitors helped me into the bedroom, brought towels from the bathroom, covered me up with my bathrobe, and then retired to the living room for a conference. I kept trying to call out to them, to speak, but somehow I could not get out a word. My teeth were chattering, it seemed, as loudly as my machine at work. The two faces returned to bend over me. I managed to grab the woman's hand and to pull her closer.

"What happened to him?" I whispered.

She stared down at me, uncomprehending for a minute. Then she understood.

"But nothing!" she said cheerfully. "What an idea! No reason to get so scared, silly!"

They explained to me that Rudolf had not yet been tried, that they had only come to take inventory, to make sure that nothing would disappear from the apartment. That way, in the event that my husband was convicted and the sentence entailed confiscation of his property, the State would sustain no loss. It was simply a routine preliminary measure, they assured me. They knew nothing about my husband's case. Then they took pains to impress upon me what an important and responsible act they were about to perform. My presence and full attention were required so that I would not be able to complain, later on, that anything was out of order. Since my state of mind clearly prevented any such attention at the moment, they would only take a rough inventory now and return the following morning. They would give me an official note to excuse me from work the following day.

I stayed in bed after they left, staring up at the ceiling. Toward evening, the bell rang again and, of course, in marched Mrs. Machova. She sized up the situation right away.

"Damned robbers!" she said. "They know how hard up for money you are and they're afraid you'll sell some of the furniture. Then there'd be nothing left for them to steal. You should have sold all of it long ago."

That was true. But I had always wanted to preserve something of a home to which Rudolf could return.

Mrs. Machova now went into the closet, pulled out our biggest suitcase, and packed up two rugs, neither one of them large but both quite valuable. They were the same rugs my mother had left with Mrs. Machova ten years earlier, before our deportation to the concentration camps.

"One pack of thieves didn't get their hands on them and a second pack should?" she grumbled. "I'll see about that."

"Don't do it," I said. "You can't carry the suitcase out of the house—the whole street is watching. If someone takes it into his head to denounce you, you'll end up in jail too."

"I'm not taking it out," she said. "I'm going to wait here until the whole house is asleep and then I'll hide it in the basement. And don't you tell those louts tomorrow that you have a place in the basement!"

Still grumbling, she moved around the other rugs to make the absence of the two she took less obvious. Then she brought two old tattered mats up from the storeroom, "just in case they counted pieces," and stuffed into the suitcases a few more things she knew

Rudolf and I were fond of: a wooden baroque candlestick, a little terracotta statue, two or three pieces of antique glass.

The next morning, I managed to pull myself together enough to help the comrades in the execution of their official duties. Their harvest was not rich. We had not accumulated any treasures in the six years that had passed since our return from the concentration camps. Under Czechoslovak law, the property of a married couple is held in common and half of it belongs to the wife. But the comrades sealed up everything except my clothes, my son's crib and his toys, and a portrait of my grandmother. Comrade inspectress, a woman well along in years, embellished her work with obscene comments and jokes directed at her colleague who was older still.

I mentioned that they were lucky: the police, at the time they had arrested Rudolf, had confiscated the keys to our car and to the garage. Otherwise, I said, I would have sold the car long before. I said this deliberately because I knew that agents of State Security had been using our car for their own purposes, driving it all over Prague. As long as the National Committee had decided to confiscate, should they not also confiscate our car? Comrade inspectress's eyes lit up. She pulled me aside and whispered, "I'll see to it that your car is released if you'll sell it to me cheap."

It was one of my rarest pleasures of the time to give her a crushing glance and to say, very loudly, "But Comrade, that would be dishonest!"

My son came back from the country tanned and healthy. It seemed to me that he had grown up a lot during those few weeks. He was reluctant to go back to nursery school and Mrs. Honzikova, the mother of his best friend in our apartment house, invited him over several times a week to spend the entire day. Her husband, a former bank employee, had been working in a factory for a long time by then.

"What else can they do to us?" she used to laugh. "Compared to all the problems I have trying to feed three kids on my husband's pay, jail would be a real vacation!"

130

She was young and pretty and she accepted life with all its trials cheerfully, like a bird in the sky. She was yet another proof to me that nothing limits a person more than what was then called "a clearly-defined world view." The people who, in my experience, proved most astute and dependable in a crisis were always those who professed the simplest ideology: love of life. Not only did they possess an instinctive ability to protect themselves from danger but they were often willing to help others as a matter of course, without ulterior motives or any heroic posturing.

The shop where I worked was located partially underground. The walls were thick and a cold dampness rose from the stone floor summer and winter alike. Early in September, the weather was still warm outside but the girls sitting at their machines were already bundled up in sweaters and shawls. None of them shivered as much as I did and, eventually, my colleagues all chipped in to buy me a pair of warm plaid carpet slippers, the kind worn by old grandmothers in the country. But not even those slippers and a heavy old sweater helped: I was still freezing.

One night after the end of my shift, I was all alone in the shop trying, once again, to catch up on my work, when I felt a flash of blinding, searing pain. I doubled up on my chair, fighting it with clenched teeth and, after a while, the pain eased. But from that time on, some lively little rodent settled inside me, a tiny mouse that gnawed and gnawed, quietly at first, but persistently.

The following Sunday, I stayed in bed but felt no better for it on Monday. There was nothing I could do except wait it out and hope it would clear up by itself. I certainly could not allow myself to get sick. Medical care was free in Czechoslovakia, and I would continue to receive part of my salary even if I were sent to a hospital. But I would not be able to continue chasing after my extra jobs, and those were the ones that made ends meet. I could not afford not to work. Not even for one week.

October came and the weather turned colder. I could barely drag myself to work. By the middle of the month, the shop erupted in anger over our working conditions, and we decided to write a piece about our grievances in the company newsletter. I was appointed to write the article. Two days after it appeared, the company manager called me into his office and proposed that I work for the newsletter on a regular basis, for a few days each month.

"We can't transfer you directly into the editorial office—surely you understand why," he said. "And we can't give you a raise. But at least you'll get away from the machine now and then and sit in a clean, warm office."

That was the first lucky break I had had in months but, by that time, I could think of nothing but how to control the constant pain. That day I had yet another surprise. As soon as I got home the telephone rang. It was my lawyer.

"A miracle has taken place," he said. "It defies all laws of nature and I can't believe it myself but it's true. I got back your savings bank passbooks. You can pick them up right away if you want."

I never found out how this miracle came to pass. Perhaps my lawyer actually did have connections and had been able to pull some strings; perhaps my remark to the inspectors about our stolen automobile had set the National Committee against State Security and someone had gotten scared. I did not know and I was not overly interested in finding out. I am always ready to believe in miracles, and this one was neither the first nor would it be the last in my life. I was completely beside myself with pain. All I understood was that my financial problems had been staved off and that I could now afford medical attention.

I knew I had to get myself into a hospital, and that was no simple matter. Medicine had become as thoroughly bureaucratized in Czechoslovakia as everything else. According to official procedure, the only doctor I could consult was our company doctor who, in turn, could refer me to a medical center or to a hospital for further treatment. But hospitals were overcrowded, and as long as one was not on the verge of dying, no doctor would write out a referral. For some time, a war had been raging between the hospitals on one side and the out-patient clinics and company doctors on the other: the overworked, underpaid clinic doctors had been sending to hospital both patients who could be cured at

132

home as well as patients who, often because of unnecessary delays, were beyond help.

Our company physician was an old woman who was herself so seriously ill and preoccupied with her own pain that she could barely bring herself to confront the ailments of others. Any patient who went to see her had to state clearly and succinctly the nature of his illness and what medication he required; she then would obligingly prescribe whatever he suggested. But anyone unable to diagnose his problem and decide upon an appropriate treatment himself was in trouble.

I decided that the situation called for a radical approach. While still in the doorway of her office, I announced that I had appendicitis, threw off my clothes without being asked, and stretched out on her examining table. When the doctor touched her cold fingertips to what was probably the only part of my body that did not hurt, I howled like a wounded animal. The poor old lady was alarmed but not alarmed enough to send me to a hospital. Instead she referred me to the surgical outpatient clinic nearest to my home where I fell into the hands of another pride of medical science, a young blonde with an oversized bun and calculating eyes.

She palpated my stomach and took my temperature without once interrupting her conversation with a nurse about some personal disagreement she had had with the director of the clinic. She told me that I had a fever of about 102 and agreed that I was probably experiencing an attack of appendicitis. But before she could send me to a hospital, I would have to go home, eat nothing and stay in bed for a day, and then return the next morning.

The next morning my temperature was 104 and the pain was becoming unbearable. I called the doctor, told her that I felt much worse, and that I could not make it to the clinic on my own. After a moment of deliberation, she said she was turning my case over to the local General Practice Clinic and that someone from there would come see me at home. She had obviously decided that if anyone had to get involved in a struggle over hospital admission, it would not be she.

Later that afternoon, an older woman doctor arrived, sat as far away from my bed as was possible without leaving the room and said there was no need to examine me. I had the flu; it was an intestinal flu that was spreading all over Prague.

"I'll give you a prescription for some pills," she said, "and you get yourself a bottle of brandy. Mix half a cup of brandy with half a cup of hot tea and drink one full cup three times a day."

Although the fever had begun to affect my thinking, I felt that these instructions were peculiar. I had been in pain for six weeks already, I objected. How could it be the flu?

"Flu is a lingering illness," she said, impatiently. "Don't flatter yourself. You're not a special case."

So Marenka went out to buy a bottle of brandy and to get the prescription filled. I started the cure.

I woke up with a start in the middle of the night. The whole room seemed to be swimming in a fluorescent blue fog. I lifted my arms and saw tiny drops of sweat form on my pores, grow larger, and then glide down my skin. My head was spinning. I thought: I have to get to the bathroom and throw some cold water on my face or else I will faint. That was my last clear thought.

Marenka found me the next morning at the other end of the apartment, sprawled out on the floor, stiff with cold. There was a large bump on my forehead where I had hit the radiator while falling.

This was the last straw for Marenka. She ran to the clinic and screamed to anyone who would listen that she was afraid to stay alone with me in the apartment, that I was liable to die at any moment and then what would she do? The doctor in charge remarked that these pampered ladies were always a pain in the neck but Marenka persisted.

"All right," the doctor said wearily. "I'll refer her to the hospital but you'll see—they'll send her packing soon enough."

I managed to put a call through to Bratislava and Marie offered to come to Prague and pick up my son the next day. Mrs. Honzikova, who had been helping us take care of Ivan from the beginning of my illness, took him into her apartment and promised to look after him until Marie arrived. I did not want my son to see me being carried out of our home on a stretcher.

Two hospital orderlies arrived that afternoon. They stared at me in disbelief and one of them said, "For God's sake, couldn't you have sent for us sooner?"

By that time, I was having trouble breathing. When Dr. Hulek at the Bulovka Hospital finally examined me, I could only answer his questions in monosyllabic whispers. He gave me a thorough physical examination and, after he had finished writing up my medical chart, the list of my ailments filled a long column which began with nephritis and ended with peritonitis. The only thing that seemed to be missing was appendicitis.

"Are you sure the doctor prescribed alcohol?" Dr. Hulek asked, several times. "The worst of it is you're so terribly run down. What on earth have you been doing with yourself? Have you ever seen the people who came back from the concentration camps?"

I nodded.

"Right now you're no better off," he said. "I'm afraid to stick a needle into you. I can't even begin to treat you until you're stronger. Give the nurse your phone number so she can call your husband or maybe your parents. She'll tell them what kind of food to bring. You won't gain much weight on what they give you here."

There was no way around it. I gathered up whatever strength I had left and explained to him, in halting whispers, why I was so terribly run down.

Dr. Hulek took exemplary care of me. But during the first few weeks I got no better, and I was tormented by worries about my child who now had no one left to support him. Father in jail, mother in hospital, no grandparents. What would happen to him if I died? Who would take care of him?

I was one of the most critical cases in the ward, and all the doctors took particular care to give me the attention I needed, especially a Dr. Wiklicka who, whenever she was on duty, prescribed special medicines to make me stronger and never failed to make some sarcastic remark about Dr. Hulek's medical prowess.

About the middle of November, still hospitalized, I received another letter from Rudolf. It was the most optimistic of all the letters he had written and the first in which he mentioned the future: "It will still be some time before I return home but we will be together again. . . ." Apparently his interrogation had ended and perhaps it had not gone as badly as I had imagined. I answered his letter with my customary tone of good cheer. I did not let him know I was ill but did write that our son was visiting his cousins in Bratislava and, for that reason, I could not enclose his monthly drawing.

Marie wrote from Bratislava: "Don't worry about Ivanek. He looks well and seems happy. He's learned several new songs here and he sings all the time."

A few days later, just as I was beginning to think I was getting better, that flash of pain struck once again, this time settling in my hip and shooting out in all directions like a burning sparkler. I could not lift my arm to reach the nurses' buzzer or even muster enough energy to cry out. It took a few minutes before the girl in the bed next to mine looked up from her book and saw me. She sounded the alarm, my bed was soon surrounded by white coats, and a syringe jabbed into my arm.

When I opened my eyes a few hours later, I thought I was still sleeping because bending over me was the blurred face of the inspector from the National Committee, the same one that had bent over me while I was regaining consciousness on the floor of my apartment. But I was not dreaming. Two men were sitting beside my bed and one of them, the inspector from the National Committee, was doggedly repeating my name.

I nodded to him to let him know I was awake and could hear him. He said that they had been trying to call the apartment and had been unable to reach anyone there. They had been ordered to bring Rudolf some shirts, a sweater, and a suit, and asked for the keys to my home. I motioned with my head to a drawer in the nightstand where I kept my handbag. The inspector pulled it out and found a bunch of keys. Through the haze of morphine I managed to ask, stupidly, "Is he coming home?"

The inspector shook his head mutely and stood there for a few minutes, staring down at me. I closed my eyes again.

I woke up with a start in the dead of night. I sat up and said out loud into the silent ward: "Trial!"

Of course! Why would they send for a suit and shirts if they were planning to send him home? A suit and shirt could mean only one thing: he was going on trial.

The night nurse came into the room with a flashlight.

"Come now," she asked. "Why aren't you sleeping?"

On November 20, 1952, the old lame woman who brought in the newspapers every morning came by as usual. The headlines on the front page swam before my eyes and an odd silence settled over the ward. THE TRIAL FOR THE ANTI-STATE CONSPIRACY OF RUDOLF SLANSKY. For God's sake, what conspiracy? I thought. Those poor people . . . At least my Rudolf could not be involved in this, thank God! He had never had anything to do with Slansky.

Then I skimmed down to the list of the accused. There were fourteen names. Eleven of them were followed by the note "of Jewish origin." Then came the words "sabotage," "espionage," "treason," like salvoes at dawn.

One of the names on the list was Rudolf Margolius. Rudolf Margolius, of Jewish origin.

With unusual clarity I heard the woman in the bed beside me whispering to her neighbor, "You have to read this—it's *Der Stuermer* all over again!" and then the voice of the lame news vendor in the corridor, "You have to read this to see how those swine sold us out to the imperialists, the bastards! They should all be hung! In public!"

Dr. Hulek appeared in the doorway, syringe in hand.

"Lie still. Don't think."

I do not know what kind of shot he gave me, but it did not

138

succeed in putting me to sleep. After a while I stumbled out to the washroom and stood there throwing up until a nurse found me and took me back to bed. Up until that day, I think, none of the women in the ward knew who I was. Now it must have become clear. If only they would not start talking about it! If only I could be alone!

Day after day, the newspapers carried detailed testimony from the accused, who not only made no attempt to defend themselves, confessing to all crimes as charged, but even kept introducing new accusations against themselves, heaping one on top of another.

Is this all or is there more you did to betray your country? Did you sell out your people to the enemy in other ways?

There is more. In my limitless hatred for the popular democratic order, I also committed the crime of . . .

Aside from the official record of the courtroom proceedings, there was other reading matter, often more shocking than the trial itself. There was the letter-to-the-editor from Lisa London, the wife of one of the three men tried who would be sentenced to life imprisonment. She wrote about a man with whom she had lived for sixteen years, with whom she had raised children and fought against the Nazis in the French Resistance, and the authenticity of her sorrow and despair was clear, "I lived with a traitor . . ."

Another letter-to-the-editor came from a child, from Ludvik Frejka's sixteen-year-old son Thomas: "I demand that my father receive the highest penalty, the death sentence . . . and it is my wish that this letter be read to him."

I cannot be sure now whether those were his exact words, but their meaning is exact. It is hard to say whose fate was more tragic, that of the father who went to his death accompanied by those words or that of the son who would have to go through life with the memory of having written them.

Every day, *Rude Pravo*, the Party newspaper, also carried commentaries on the trials from the pens of various intellectuals. Some were incompetent hacks such as Ivan Skala, a so-called poet whose sole claim to immortality lies in the vulgarity of his outbursts against the accused, and whose article about Rudolf ended with the line,

"To a dog, a dog's death!" But even noted, respected writers such as Karel Konrad, Ivan Obracht, and Jarmila Glazerova volunteered their poisonous opinions.

The women on my ward kept silent. At night I would sneak out of bed and huddle on a bench in the corridor by myself. Eventually the nurses got used to it and stopped trying to get me to go back to bed. Occasionally one of them would drape a blanket over my shoulders. I could feel the quiet hospital simmering with hatred. What could it be like, how much worse would it be, outside?

Then one night I heard a nurse speaking behind a partially closed door.

"Back home in my village," she was saying, "when a thief stole a goose, he denied he had done it to the end—even if he had been caught red-handed. These poor people are standing up confessing to all kinds of horrible crimes and accusing themselves of things nobody's even asked them about! Who knows what they did to them? The whole thing stinks to high heaven!"

On the fifth day of the trial, Rudolf was slated to testify. I could not stand the tension in the hospital anymore. When Dr. Hulek made his rounds that morning, I begged him to send me home. He would not hear of it.

"I know how you feel," he said. "But I can't in good conscience do it. You're still listed in critical condition. It's absolutely out of the question to discharge you."

The trial in its entirety was being broadcast over the radio. I waited in the corridor until the nurse whom I had overheard talking the night before came in and pleaded with her to let me listen in her private room. Reluctantly, she agreed. That evening, she picked me up in a wheelchair and took me there.

Up until that evening, I had managed to hold on to a glimmer of hope. Rudolf was the only man on trial who was not a veteran Communist; he had joined the Party only after the war. He had never been part of the group around Slansky; he had never held a high position in the Party. There were many other ways in which he did not fit into the group of the accused.

And then, after almost a year, I heard his voice.

As soon as he began to speak, I knew things were very bad.

140

He spoke in such an odd, tense, monotonous voice that, at first, I thought he had been drugged. Then I realized that he was simply reciting something he had memorized. A few times he stopped short, as though he were trying to remember his lines, and then he started up again, like a robot.

The things he said! First about his parents, then about himself, finally about his work. Lie after lie. He had joined the Party only in order to betray it. He had devoted his energies to nothing but espionage and sabotage. He had enriched himself by taking bribes and, as a mercenary in the employ of the imperialists, he had plotted far-reaching conspiracies against the Republic and its people.

Then came the unfortunate trade agreement with England, for which he had received the congratulations of Gottwald himself. This had now been transformed into the most treacherous act of his career, an act of sabotage which had dealt a near-fatal blow to the Czechoslovak economy.

How could they have forced him to such testimony, my Rudolf who had never, in all the years I had known him, ever lied about anything? How could they have made him vilify his parents, who had been murdered in Auschwitz? What had he suffered before he broke down? How had they crushed him? At one point, I heard Rudolf's voice say that he had been trained in espionage in London during the war when, of course, he had spent the entire war as a prisoner in German concentration camps. This item was dutifully reported in the Party newspaper the following day, but later edited out of a book in which the transcript of the trial was published.

Toward the end of the broadcast, I could no longer take it in. The nurse wheeled me back into my ward without a word.

The next morning, Dr. Hulek had me brought into his office. He looked at me unhappily. "Please forgive me," he said. "But I've received an order to discharge you immediately. It's a terrible thing to do. You still are in serious need of hospital care. But I don't have the power to keep you here. I have to obey orders."

"Don't worry," I said. "I'll be better off at home. But could you send me in an ambulance?"

"I'm so sorry. Unfortunately . . ."

Later I learned what had happened. The Party had ordered general meetings of employees at all institutions and enterprises, including the hospitals, where a resolution had been read demanding the death penalty for all those accused in what came to be known as the Slansky Trial. At the hospital where I was a patient, the vote was taken by a show of hands, and Dr. Hulek alone did not raise his hand in favor of the resolution.

That did not escape the attention of the comrades. Among the most vehement was Dr. Wicklicka, the physician who had shown me such concern until she discovered my identity. She had attacked Dr. Hulek in public, accusing him of keeping me in the hospital to shield me from the rightful wrath of the people, thereby helping an enemy of the Party and of the working class. This was such a dangerous accusation that even the chief surgeon became frightened. Poor Dr. Hulek, a mere staff physician and the father of three children, had no choice but to act on their orders.

I went back to my ward and slowly started packing. Within a few minutes I had fallen back onto my bed, soaked with sweat. How on earth would I get home? They had brought me to the hospital in an ambulance, dressed in a robe, covered with a blanket. I had no dress, no stockings, no shoes, not even a coat. Outside it was winter. My usual salvation, Mrs. Machova, was lying in another hospital, herself seriously ill. This time I would not have dared to call her anyhow. She had a husband and a child. Finally I remembered the former secretary of my first publisher, an elderly single woman who had always been kind to me. She was now retired and had no family to protect. This was someone I would probably not hurt. I called to feel her out. She agreed to pick me up in a taxi and to bring along an old coat and a pair of shoes.

The trip home sapped all my remaining energy. In order to manage the few steps from the front door to the elevator, I had to crawl on all fours. But when I finally lay down in my own bed, I felt relieved. I no longer had to pretend. I no longer had to control my anxiety. At last I was alone. I could prepare for whatever was coming.

The trial of the fourteen men took only one week. Now it was over and everyone waited for the verdict. On November 27, I got up in the morning, put on Rudolf's robe, and shuffled into the abandoned nursery. I lay down on Ivan's bed and switched on the radio. By that time I had become totally oblivious to the things around me, to myself, even to the pain that had returned in full force. And then a voice spurted out of the radio set, flooding the room from floor to ceiling until it forced out the last glimmer of light, the last bubble of air.

"In the trial of the Anti-State Conspiracy . . . Rudolf Slansky, death penalty . . . Vlado Clementis, death penalty . . . Ludvik Frejka, death penalty . . . death penalty . . . death penalty . . . Rudolf Margolius, death penalty."

I do not know how long I lay there, motionless, without a thought, without pain, in total emptiness.

At the same moment Marie was sitting by her radio set in Bratislava, in the kitchen, with her mother. Her children, Ivan, and a few friends from the neighborhood were playing noisily at the other end of the apartment. A different voice came from her radio set, but the words were the same. Marie's old, ailing mother cried out. None of the other children noticed. Only Rudolf's son came to the door of the kitchen and asked, anxiously, "What happened?"

"Nothing," said Marie. "Grandmother wasn't feeling well. But she's better now. Go back and play."

Ivan looked at her seriously and said, "I'm so glad. I got scared. I thought someone had died."

The doorbell rang and rang. I lay on Ivan's bed without moving. I could hear the sound quite clearly but I did not understand what it meant. It was as though my brain did not know what to do with the information that my senses registered. It was a long time before I slipped down from the bed and crawled, inch by inch, to the door. I reached up for the doorknob.

Pavel Eisler stood in the doorway. He bent down, picked me up, and carried me into the bedroom. Then the bell rang again. This time it was the composer Jan Hanus, who was Rudolf's closest friend. It had always seemed to me that there was a kinship between the two men that could not be explained by friendship alone. They were like two houses built in different styles but of the same stone. Jan sat down at the foot of the bed and spoke to me quietly. I could not take in the words, only the soothing melody of his voice and the expression of his kind, beautiful face.

The telephone on the night table rang. It was the lawyer.

"Mr. Bartos," I gasped. "How is it possible—"

"But Mrs. Margolius, what did you expect? After all, your husband confessed."

Rudolf . . . Rudolf . . .

I hardly remember anything of the week that followed the sentencing. In my bedroom it was always night. Only now and then

144

a face came moving toward me out of the darkness, a few words. Dr. Padovcova's hand holding a syringe that erased everything for a few hours. . . . the voices of two comrades from the shop where I worked, "You are fired effective immediately . . ." the shocked face of Karlicek, our farmer friend, and his voice, "That woman is on her last legs. What will happen to the child?" . . . and once, unexpectedly, a man in an Army uniform, Pavel Kovaly, who had gone AWOL in order to come see me.

On the evening of December 2, two men appeared in my bedroom. I recognized one of them as the agent who used to take my letters to Rudolf. He said, "You have a last opportunity to speak with your husband, but if you are too ill to come with us, stay in bed. We'll just leave."

I began to scream. I begged them not to leave, to wait for me, to give me a minute; then I would be ready to go. They looked at each other, then one of them said, "All right," and they went out to sit in the next room.

I tried to hurry up but things slipped out of my hands as though I had lost the ability to coordinate my movements. When, finally, I was dressed, I was trembling so hard that I fell back down on my bed. The agents came back into my bedroom, held me up by my elbows and led me, step by step, to the car waiting in front of the house.

I looked out the window and saw Prague covered with snow, the streets deserted. It was a long ride. We stopped at a side entrance of the courthouse in Pankrac where the two men helped me out of the car and led me down a long corridor to a tiny cubicle. There they ordered me to wait. Voices filtered through the thin gray wall. In the next room, probably a cubicle just like mine, a woman was talking excitedly, resentfully, as if arguing with someone. "I don't want to talk to him. He's a traitor; he deceived all of us. Even me. I have nothing to say to him!"

"Mrs. Frejka," a man's voice said, probably the voice of the security agent, "Mrs. Frejka, be human. That man is going to die tomorrow . . ."

Just then the door flew open and the two agents again pulled me up by my arms and led me into a larger room, empty, and divided in half by a double barrier of wire mesh. Then, behind that fence, two policemen appeared with Rudolf between them.

I threw myself onto the wire mesh and hooked my fingers through the loops. I saw Rudolf's face crisscrossed by the wire pattern as though by a tissue of scars. But then, in just moments, the black web began to dissolve. I looked straight into his eyes and saw no despair, no fear, only a strange, distant calm. It was the calm a man finds only at the very bottom of suffering.

He looked at me for a long time before he spoke. Then he said, "I was so afraid you wouldn't come!"

I could not utter a word. Are you already so far away from me Rudolf that you could imagine that I would not come?

He kept looking at me silently. I thought: What must I look like to him? Skin and bones, worn out by illness and pain.

"You're so beautiful," he said.

"Tell me about Ivan," he asked, and I started to talk. I told him everything I could think of about our handsome, cheerful little son who sang all day long.

After a while we were both smiling.

"Today I had a long conversation with Minister of State Security Bacilek," Rudolf said. "He promised he'd take care of you and the child, that he'd get you a good job, that he'd help . . . And now listen, this is important: I want you to have the boy's name changed. He must not be made to suffer on my account. Don't argue with me. Just do it. It's my last wish."

We were silent again. Then he said, "Come, let's have a cigarette together."

A security agent leaped to my side with a cigarette and a lighter.

"You know," said Rudolf, "I've been sharing a cell with a man who loves music as much as I do. We've been trying to remember together and now we can whistle the entire Dvořak cello concerto."

We smoked for a while without saying anything, looking at each other.

"Don't question the trial. Believe it!" Rudolf said suddenly. "Please. Think of Ivan, not of me."

146

"Don't say anything. I understand it all. Don't worry about me or the boy. I'll raise him well, I promise you. I'll bring him up to be a good man."

"And forget me, Heda. Find him a new father. Don't stay alone."

"I know I have to take care of the child but, believe me, I'd rather go with you. . . . It would be easier than living. . . . I'm with you anyway. You know that, don't you?"

"Have you noticed that all the important events of my life have taken place either on the third or thirteenth of the month?" asked Rudolf. "Tomorrow is the third and I'm three times thirteen years old."

"Three times thirteen hard years," I said. "But you had at least one good thing: a woman who always loved you and believed in you."

I paused, then turned to the agent who was standing beside me and said, "I've brought my husband photographs of our child. Can you give them to him?"

"That's prohibited."

"Won't you allow us even to shake hands?"

"That's prohibited."

I stretched a finger through the wire barrier as far as I could, trying to touch Rudolf's hand, but could not reach it. Rudolf smiled.

We spoke a while longer, with a growing awareness of each passing minute. One of the uniformed policemen on Rudolf's side looked at his watch. Rudolf nodded.

"I just wanted to tell you one more thing," he said hurriedly. "I read a good book while I was here. It was called *Men of Clear Conscience*."

I do not know whether he said anything after that. All I could understand was that these were our last moments, the very last.

Rudolf backed away toward the door and, just as he stepped through it, the expression in his eyes changed suddenly, and what appeared in them for that brief moment I will carry within me as long as I live.

When the door closed, my knees gave way. I hung by my fingers from the wire mesh and one of the agents bent over to catch me before I fell. But he had barely touched me when something inside me rebelled. I broke away from him and marched, ramrod straight, through all those corridors and out to the waiting car. When we arrived at my house, I got out of the car myself and walked up to our apartment alone.

Then came the night. All that night long, a huge hammer kept moving before my eyes, hammering a splash of blood to a stone wall with regular strokes, pounding down, pounding down. . . .

Before dawn, I fell asleep for a few minutes just at the time, I later learned, that Rudolf was dying without a single word.

More than thirty years have now passed and that night is still not over. It remains to this day as a screen onto which my present life is projected. I measure all my happiness and all my misfortunes against it, in the way that the height of mountains and the depth of valleys are measured against the level of the sea.

I have asked myself more than once: What if Rudolf had died of some protracted illness? What if he had been suffering for months on end from intolerable physical pain with both of us knowing, as we knew then, that he had to die? Would it have been any easier? I think so. We all can bear the pain that comes from being flesh and blood, transients, doomed to die. But it is impossible to be reconciled to suffering that man inflicts in cold blood on his fellow man.

After Rudolf's death, I spent several weeks lying in my bed as though it were a coffin. The streets of Prague were seething with rage. Rumor had it that I had been kidnapped together with my child and taken abroad, that I was in jail, that I had committed suicide. The truth was that there was not much life left in me. Once a doctor from the local clinic came to have a look at me, examined me as though he were impatient to get away, and said, "This is a difficult thing. You aren't resisting the illness. You don't really want to live."

That was not true. I knew I had to live. I had to take care of my son. But I had no strength left, and every day I felt worse. Then one night my landlady, regretting her former cruelty perhaps, showed up in my bedroom with a Dr. Urbanek, a physician whom I had never met before. He gave me a thorough examination and then said, "I'm going to prescribe a rather risky treatment but it's the only thing that might work. If it doesn't help, you'll have to go back to the hospital. Otherwise. . . ."

He wrote out a few prescriptions and then sneaked out as furtively as he had come. I found out later that he had been transferred to a position somewhere far out in the country, I hope not as a punishment for having saved my life. Marenka had to walk all over Prague for days before she had all the prescriptions filled, but from the time I began to take the medication, my illness was arrested and began its retreat, although it would be a year before I would be well again.

Sometime during this period I received the news that I had been expelled from the Party.

A few weeks later, I was able to walk again. I decided that I would go outside dressed only in mourning. I could not afford to buy anything new, but I found an old black coat in the closet and a pair of black shoes. Marenka and I dyed everything else. Dozens of spiteful stares followed me as I shuffled along the sidewalk, stopping every now and then to lean against a wall and catch my breath. I knew that I might be assaulted, that a stone might come hurtling toward me, because that had already happened to some of the widows and children of the executed. But, much to my surprise, I began to sense for the first time that my street had split into two camps.

Much later, a woman told me, "You know, people aren't all that mean. It's just that they don't think. To gang up on a public enemy is a deep-rooted custom of the country, almost a national tradition. But people have a completely different reaction to a widow in mourning, especially if she looks as wretched as you did then. And once they start opening their minds, there's no stopping the process. It began to dawn on some people that had you not been absolutely sure of your husband's innocence, you wouldn't have had the guts to challenge the Party by wearing mourning for him."

No one dared socialize with me, to be sure, but I could observe the reactions of the people at our local clinic where the doctors reluctantly agreed to give me some attention and an occasional prescription.

One of the saddest phenomena of that time was the reemergence of anti-Semitism which usually remains buried deep below the surface in Bohemia and erupts only in response to a signal from above. I remember a conversation I overheard at the clinic. Two old women were talking about their respective illnesses, as is usual in the waiting rooms of doctors.

"I tell you, I was *so* sick," said one of them, "and they sent me from one doctor to another and none of them helped me a bit until that one. He fixed me up in no time. He took such good care of me that if it hadn't been for him I'd be six feet under by now!"

"Really? What kind of doctor was he?" asked her listener.

"Oh, you know, one of those dirty Jews."

In late January, Marie brought Ivan back to Prague. She had guessed, correctly, that we needed each other now more than anything else. The children of the comrades in Bratislava had been strictly forbidden to play with the son of a traitor, and the boy had begun to feel lonely. But he looked healthy, spoke Czech with a soft Slovak accent, and seemed to me even more precious than before. He was a little startled when he first saw me but said nothing and went to check up on his toys. It was only later that he came over to me and asked, "Mama, why are you wearing black clothes? They're ugly. They make you look sad."

I sat him down beside me and, very carefully, told him that his father had died.

He listened and looked frightened, but he did not cry.

"Where's he buried?" he asked. "I'd like to plant a flower for him there."

I told him that his father had died in a foreign country, far away.

"When you grow up," I said, "we'll go there to see his grave."

He went into his room, puttered around for a while, and came back.

"Don't worry, Mama," he said, "I've already grown up a lot. I'll take care of you."

As soon as I could stand on my feet long enough to cross a few streets, I went to the police precinct. I pulled my citizen's identity card out of my handbag and asked for a correction of my status. The entry "married" now needed to be changed to "widowed." The pudgy young policeman looked first at me, then at my card and said, "All right. Show me your husband's death certificate."

The official death certificate was precisely what I wanted.

"I did not receive one," I said.

"Then at least the court verdict."

"I didn't receive that either," I said. "I learned about the trial and the verdict from the radio and the papers, just like everybody else."

"But that's impossible!" exclaimed the policeman. "You have the right by law to. . . ." By that time one of his superiors had stepped up and nudged him in the side with his elbow. The young policeman stopped in mid-sentence.

"Go to the National Committee," said the older man. "Ask them to issue you a death certificate."

I went to the National Committee's local office a few blocks away.

"Certainly," replied the clerk there. "May I have the coroner's report?"

"I didn't receive one."

"No one can issue you a death certificate without proof of death."

"Then what should I do?"

The clerk squirmed with embarrassment. "You know what you can do? Go see the people over at the Central National Committee."

By that time I had learned to distinguish between bureaucrats and human beings at a glance. The man behind the desk at the Central National Committee was a human being. I sat down to explain the situation.

"I know all about it already," he said. "A death certificate cannot be issued without a coroner's report. And no coroner's reports have been issued for any of the men who were executed."

My heart started to pound.

"Do you think it's possible that they're still alive?"

The man shrugged.

"Anything's possible these days. Don't run around anymore. Save your strength. Here, sign a written request. That'll give me an excuse to investigate the matter. Call me in a week."

Weeks and months went by. The answer to my inquiry was always, "Nothing so far."

Why were they refusing to come up with a death certificate? Had the trial been some bizarre comedy? Was Rudolf still alive? Was it possible that they were all being interned somewhere? That when the trial had served its purpose the Party had decided to spare the lives of the innocent after all? Friends advised me not to get my hopes up, but I could not help thinking . . . who knows . . . maybe. . . .

I received the death certificate two years later. It is a unique document.

Date of death: December 3, 1952

Date of issue: January 5, 1955

Occupation of deceased: Deputy Minister

Cause of death: Suffocation by hanging

Place of Burial:_____

This last point would be clarified twenty years later.

I learned then that the bodies had been cremated and the ashes turned over to two members of State Security for disposal. They drove in an official limousine and its driver supposedly made a joke. "This is the first time I've packed fourteen people into this car," he said. "The three of us—and those eleven in the bag."

A few miles out of Prague, the limousine began to skid on the icy road. The agents got out and scattered the ashes under its wheels.

J anuary, 1953 marked the beginning of the tug of war for my apartment.

The Ministry sent over a pleasant young man whose name I have forgotten, and a fat middle-aged spinster by the name of Vokurkova, which means pickle in Czech. Comrade Pickle looked over the apartment without much interest but focused her attention on me. She had apparently decided that all I needed to heal my ailing body was a good dose of her militant Bolshevik vigor and revolutionary spirit. She stood in the middle of my kitchen in all her magnitude and delivered herself of an impassioned speech.

"The only thing that can keep you alive now is hate," she declared. "Your husband was a traitor and a rat and you should hate him for it! You must repeat to yourself every day: I hate him; I hate him; I hate him. You'll see how much strength that will give you. Women always think it's love that moves mountains, but nothing can beat hatred for giving you strength!"

I started trembling, and the young man took my arm, leading me out of the room.

"For heaven's sake, don't listen to that old bag," he said. "She's just a sour old maid. You were always a thorn in her side, even though she never spoke to you before. Don't believe a word she says. All of us at the Ministry are convinced your husband was innocent. I know that our section chief Hrubis was interrogated and testified very bravely on his behalf."

154

Before they left, Comrade Pickle informed me that higher authorities had decided to move me out of Prague to a nearby village where I would be assigned "a whole cottage" to myself.

Mrs. Machova, who was still convalescing from her illness, offered to go out with me to look it over. It was a long trip. When we finally reached our destination in the cold and snow, we discovered that the comrade's information had been inaccurate—the cottage was anything but "whole."

It was a dilapidated hut which had been condemned long before. There was no electricity. The plaster had fallen off the walls, which were damp from floor to ceiling. There was no plumbing. Water would have to be carried up the quarter-mile slope of a steep hill from a neighbor's well. "If the neighbors allow it," according to the rustic old man who served as the secretary of the local National Committee.

There was no possibility of employment in the area. It was clear that under these circumstances my son and I would not have survived more than a few months. There are various ways to commit murder.

On the train back to Prague, Mrs. Machova came up with a solution.

"The only way you can lick this," she said, "is to get the local National Committee to give you a letter stating that the shack is designated for demolition according to the Five-Year Plan. That Plan is sacred. They won't let anything interfere with it. You write to that lout of a secretary that you want to talk it over with him but that you're too ill to come back out here and could he please come see you in Prague. We'll write up the letter ahead of time and buy a bottle of booze. You'll keep filling up his glass until he signs and then you mail it yourself, right to the Ministry. And don't fret. There's nothing crooked about it. It's all true. And I could see for myself that they didn't seem too happy about having you in their village anyway!"

That is exactly how it happened. The secretary of the local National Committee came, drank, and signed. I believe that a load fell off his chest when he got rid of me. A few days later, I received a message from the Ministry—they would be assigning me to other quarters. Marenka moved out; the local National Committee assigned her a room elsewhere.

Then came the Comrade Inspectors from the National Committee in my own neighborhood, who announced that they would return shortly to remove the property they had inventoried for confiscation. They advised me to file a petition for the release of the most basic personal necessities.

My petition was granted. I was allowed to keep a bed, a table, two chairs, cups, plates, and cutlery for two people, and some pots and pans for the kitchen.

The removal of our personal property went ahead without a hitch, except for one detail. I had told Ivan that we were going to move to a smaller apartment and that I was selling everything we did not need. He understood, but begged me not to sell the radio which I had bought for the last Christmas that Rudolf and Ivan and I were together. Ivan had fallen in love with that radio and spent hours playing with all the buttons he could push and turn.

I opened up negotiations with the Comrade Inspectors. I had bought the radio myself, I said, with my own money and I had documents to prove it. I was not protesting the illegal confiscation of my other property, but I wanted to keep my radio. Comrade Inspector deliberated for some time and then said that this was a matter beyond his jurisdiction. He decided to put the case before the highest authority and called the public prosecutor, who gave him the following opinion:

"Of course she has a legal right to it! But if she has the nerve to press a claim, let her sue us! Just let her try it and she'll find out a thing or two!"

When Comrade Inspector repeated this reply from the man who was the guardian of law and order in our country, he blushed to the roots of his hair.

I noticed at about that time that the doctor at my neighborhood clinic who certified me as disabled every week was becoming more and more nervous. It seemed that he too had received orders not to coddle me but, at the same time, he could not ignore the fact that my condition was still very poor. I knew that as soon as he

156

declared me capable of work the Labor Office would lose no time in finding me. The charge of parasitism was once again hanging over my head, but who would employ me now?

By chance, I stumbled across a peculiar enterprise. It was located in a small basement littered with discarded cotton wool scraps and various kinds of thread, and run by an elderly man whom I never saw without his winter coat and hat. He passed out tiny hand looms along with armfuls of scraps which the employees took home and wove into ugly, but warm scarves. Most of these people were retired or handicapped and needed to supplement their pensions with a little pocket money. It was impossible to earn more than pocket money this way, even if you worked for twenty-four hours a day, but it was employment. It provided shelter from the Labor Office and the charge of parasitism.

While I was busy weaving scarves, humanity suffered a horrendous loss. Father Stalin, the man of genius, the leader of all peoples, died. I too did my mourning. I mourned sincerely that this tragic event had not taken place six months earlier, at a time when it might have saved Rudolf.

Not long after, it was reported in the press that the conviction of a group of Jewish doctors who had recently been sentenced to death in the Soviet Union had been reversed. The report added, laconically, that their confessions had been extracted by illegal means.

I sat down at once to write a letter to the Central Committee in which I swore that my husband was as innocent as those doctors. I suggested that he had confessed as a result of similar illegal methods of interrogation. Then I made a formal request for a review of his trial. Once again, there was no answer.

About a month later, obedient as ever, Comrade Klement Gottwald followed Iosif Vissarionovich into eternity. He passed away quietly. It was rumored that the cause of death was an aneurism of the aorta, precipitated by advanced syphilis. The circumstances of his death were quite moving, although, of course, considerably less so than those of Stalin's. After all, we are a much smaller country.

157

We acquired our second workers' president, Comrade President Antonin Zapotocky. All that changed was that the new president did not drink his beer quietly and in private as Gottwald had done. He liked to mix with the crowds and to play cards noisily and publicly with the soldiers of the palace guard.

The Party also got a new General Secretary, Antonin Novotny, a man of the future who had won the trust and esteem of the Party primarily by unmasking the Anti-State Conspiracy of Rudolf Slansky and his associates. That had not been an easy job, he would later complain to his friends. "Gottwald just refused to believe me. You have no idea how hard it was to convince him these people were traitors."

There were some changes in my life too.

The Ministry of Foreign Trade finally succeeded in finding me a place to live. They must have scoured the city, because in all of Prague there could have been at best a handful of such hovels. It was a single room with an ancient brick oven in one corner. The floorboards were broken and the window frames and door so rotted out that whenever the wind blew, anything light would start to fly around the room, even with the windows closed. The house was at least three hundred years old. Our only modern conveniences were a bare electric bulb in the room, and a dripping cold water faucet and an indescribable toilet in the hall that were shared by several families on the floor. No other hygienic facility had penetrated the building.

I put a crate filled with coal in one corner of the room and a large box filled with potatoes and other food in another. I stretched ropes across the ceiling to serve as clothes lines for the laundry which I washed in what had been the baby bassinet. That bassinet also served as our bathtub.

Pavel Kovaly appeared once again with a tiny cannon stove he had managed to scrounge up somewhere, together with several lengths of pipe. He fitted these ingeniously across the room so that every bit of heat could be captured. Unfortunately, the stove only gave off heat when it was full of glowing coals. As soon as the fire died down, the room would become an icebox. Ivan and I always

158

raced up and down the incredibly dirty staircase with our eyes half closed so that we would not see the cockroaches, almost as large as mice, that were crawling up the walls.

Before we could move in, I had to see the landlord to sign a lease. He was a very old sick man in a wheelchair, who scrutinized my application through his spectacles for a long time before he looked up.

"Your name is Margolius," he said finally. "You wouldn't happen to be related to the one that was hanged, would you?"

Silently I thought, Forgive me Rudolf, please forgive me, but I cannot take any more. . . .

"No," I said.

"Well you're lucky," said the landlord and nodded his white head.

My son kept his word. He helped me with everything. Because I continued to be ill on and off for another year, he did the housework when I had to stay in bed. Often, I would hear the noise of children playing downstairs in the street while he was washing the dishes or scrubbing the floor. At the age of six, he was more mature and responsible than many an adult. He rarely asked for anything. On the contrary, he would always insist that he was fine and needed nothing. I remember only one evening when he said wistfully, "All the children in school bring such beautiful red apples for lunch. . . ." But that was precisely at a time when even a few of those apples were an impossible dream.

Today Ivan lives in London. He is a successful architect and has written an interesting book on art. The buildings he designs have great strength and beauty, and a quiet, serene dignity. He, his wife, and his two children are citizens of Great Britain, the world's oldest democracy.

In the spring of 1953, the long-feared currency reform was finally enacted. The currency was devalued at the rate of fifty to one, reducing the tiny remnant of my savings to almost nothing. At that point, I panicked. If I should not be able to hold onto my job, miserable though it was, we would starve to death.

159

Then I had an idea. I would volunteer for an agricultural brigade on one of the state-run farms which recruited volunteers for the summer. That would earn me points at work, and my son would be out in the fresh air. I would manage the work somehow. My former neighbor, Mrs. Honzikova, offered me a room at her mother's house in a village where there was a large state farm, and I went to see the manager of the scarf enterprise.

His face lit up when I told him my plans.

"I'll report this higher up right away," he said. "Since all the rest of our workers are either old geezers or invalids, you'll be our only volunteer, the pride of the establishment. You'll be all set now. You won't have to worry about holding onto your job next year."

The first six weeks, as we turned the hay and weeded the carrots, everything went well. But then came harvesting and, along with it, the back-breaking work that once again set off a bout of illness. There was no alternative but to return to Prague. A young and sympathetic physician at the clinic examined me and then burst out, "Tell me what doctor certified you fit for field work! I'll file a complaint against him right away!"

It took some doing to calm her down. Afterward, I went to the basement workshop to announce my return but this time my boss did not hand me the usual bundle of scraps. He shuffled his feet, cleared his throat, and averted his eyes. Finally he said, "Two weeks ago, I received an order to fire you. I should have written, but I kept postponing it. I felt sorry for you . . ."

As soon as I felt better, I started job hunting again, even though I knew it was useless. Some of the personnel directors, who would not have dreamed of hiring me for anything, had a good time playing games at my expense. They sat me down across from their desks, shone a strong light in my face, and posed a series of intricate questions. In my fierce attempt to look innocent, I must have looked as though I had committed a mass murder. But then how does an innocent person actually look?

My job hunt lasted one week. When the personnel director of a dental clinic where I had applied for a job as a cleaning woman

160

said to me, "What can you be thinking of, Comrade? You can't work here! We have very high political standards!" I decided, enough! I'm not putting up with any more of this. This is the end.

My friends helped me out as much as they could. One would bring over a short translation; another, some proof-reading or an order for an illustration. Pavel Kovaly, who had completed his military service and was back at the publishing house where I used to work, had the nerve to tell the editor-in-chief that he had learned how to draw in the army. From time to time he would bring me an order for a book jacket and then sign the design himself.

But all of this brought in pitifully little money, and I began to wonder whether I was really as indispensable to my son as I had thought. As long as I was alive, he was condemned to unending deprivation and misery. If I died, Marie or Mrs. Machova would certainly take him in, and then he would grow up in a tolerable environment, in a decent apartment, within a family. I mulled this possibility over and over, until one day when I returned home later than usual from yet another search for work, and Ivan came running to me, terrified.

"Where were you so long Mama? I was afraid something had happened to you!"

I thought that this was a good opportunity to feel him out. First I calmed him down and promised that nothing would happen to me, that I was very careful. Then I added, "But even if something should ever happen to me, you'd go live with Aunt Marie and maybe you'd have a better time living there than here with me!"

Ivan stared at me in amazement with Rudolf's eyes.

"But then I wouldn't have my own mother!"

I took him into my arms and held him tight, more ashamed of myself than I had ever before been in my life.

Then one morning the inspector from the Labor Department arrived. She sat down at our table, pulled out a file and a questionnaire and said, "I've come to investigate how you make a living. You've been unemployed since August."

That made me so mad that I exploded.

161

"I don't feel like working. I have a rich lover who keeps me!"

The woman looked at me sadly. "Listen, I understand. Don't think I like doing this. But I have to file some kind of report on you. I want to protect you. Be sensible."

I pulled out a folder with several drawings in it, most of them more than three years old. "Write in your report that I work as a freelance artist," I said. "Here's some of my work."

Somehow we survived that first winter in our hovel. The second one was worse. Every morning we had to break the crust of ice that had formed overnight in the water pitcher. My health once again took a turn for the worse, and Ivan, too, began getting sick.

One day Pavel Kovaly came to visit. He stopped in the door, speechless. I was lying in my bed, Ivan in his. We both had the flu and high fever. It was as cold inside our room as it was out on the street, and a few pieces of paper were blowing around, propelled by the north wind. I had not had enough strength to start a fire in the stove, let alone to go downstairs and walk several blocks to a telephone booth to call a doctor. Pavel took a blanket, wrapped it around Ivan, and carried him to Mrs. Machova. Then he came back, wrapped me up in a blanket, and carried me to his mother.

Several weeks later, Pavel and I were married. It was an odd wedding. This time the bridegroom had the flu and shivered throughout the ceremony. I was so upset that I could barely stand up myself. The few friends who had dared to come wept. Pavel Eisler was my witness and of course Mrs. Machova was there too. After the ceremony, we all dug into our pockets, pooled what we found, and went to the Cafe Pelikan for coffee and cake.

Naturally our marriage cost Pavel Kovaly his job. In the months that followed, he helped build socialism underground as an unskilled laborer, assisting a man who fixed water heaters. Since at the time it mattered less how well a man worked, and more how good he was at cheating and falsifying reports, Pavel often earned next to nothing.

The three of us moved into his mother's two-room apartment and were relieved when Pavel found another job in a large bakery

162

from which he sometimes managed to smuggle home a couple of rolls for Ivan.

By then 1956 was drawing closer, a year of great revelations and small changes.

In February, 1956, a new era began. Nikita Khrushchev, who had long been involved in a power struggle at the Kremlin, had realized that a bold act was needed to strengthen his position. Being a shrewd politician, he also saw that the time was ripe for breaking away from the barbarity of Stalinist rule. In a secret speech delivered to a closed session of the Twentieth Congress of the Soviet Communist Party, Khrushchev cast the first stone at the God-like image of Stalin and disclosed some of Stalin's worst crimes. It was only a crack in the wall of terror which Stalin and his henchmen had built, but it was enough to save hundreds of thousands of innocent lives. Political prisoners, some of whom had been rotting in jails and labor camps for many years, were released in all countries of the Soviet Bloc.

In Czechoslovakia, the prison gates opened quietly, unobtrusively, and through them walked shattered, emaciated people, blinking their eyes in the daylight. They came back to find their homes destroyed, their wives sick and exhausted, their children strangers to them. Former friends avoided them, not out of fear any more, but out of shame and embarrassment. Their health was ruined or gravely damaged; some died shortly after their return. It often took months before they could find housing and work. State Security kept them under constant observation lest they hurt themselves by recounting too vividly what they had experienced in the prisons.

I first saw Eda Goldstuecker after his release at Pavel Eisler's home. He had become so small and skinny that he looked like a young boy. He stared at us and at everything around him with a thirsty rapture, as though he were comparing what he saw to what he had been imagining for all those years and was now amazed at how much more beautiful reality had turned out to be than the most accurate memory.

Among those released were Artur London, Eugen Loebl, and Vavro Hajdu, the three of the fourteen men accused of conspiracy in the Slansky trial who, for reasons that never came to light, escaped the death sentence and were given life imprisonment. Now they were released and rehabilitated without a word of explanation. Because they were alive, they were declared innocent. The dead remained traitors, even though the accusations against the whole group were so intertwined that if one were declared innocent, none could be guilty. Nevertheless, in 1957, a special commission appointed by the Party and headed by Rudolf Barak ostensibly reexamined the transcripts of the trials and concluded that they had been conducted in strict accordance with the law and had served the goals of the Party.

But in those few months after Khrushchev exploded his bomb, and before the Party regained its bearings and tightened the screws once again, most people saw the light. Millions waited, expecting that any day now our Party would finally speak out. We wanted to know the truth and we wanted to hear the truth spoken out loud. But what was the truth? In 1956 in Czechoslovakia, the truth was still whatever served the needs of the Party and the Party meant Comrade Novotny and his allies, inseparably bound together by their crimes. No revelations were forthcoming, and the country, which had just begun to recover from the paralysis of fear, sank into a morass of unspoken guilt and shame.

Society became polarized between those who wielded power—a power that had become self-sufficient and independent of the will of the people—and all other mortals. A similar split ran through every other aspect of life. Even the thoughts of most individuals became divided into private and public compartments, and the two often had nothing in common. During the day, people put in their hours at work and fulfilling their Party obligations; then they went home, removed their masks, and began to live for a few hours. Lying and play acting became a way of life; indifference and apathy became its essence. Even small children knew not to repeat in school what had been said at home; they learned not to display interest in anything, to become involved with nothing.

Our own situation improved gradually. My husband, who had a degree in philosophy, managed to get an appointment at the Academy of Sciences through the intervention of friends. I acquired my first major translating assignment. Rather symbolically, it happened to be Arnold Zweig's novel *The Case of Sergeant Grischa*, a story of an innocent man destroyed by the machinery of power.

I have often pondered the devious route that led me to my real vocation. Were it not for my misfortunes, I would probably have spent my life doing illustrations, which were, at best, mediocre. After having translated the first chapter of my first book, I realized with amazement and humility that I was doing what I had been born to do. Enthralled by the beauty of the exact word which blends flawlessly with a clearcut idea, I entered a new world, the company of my authors. And what company it was! John Steinbeck, William Golding, Heinrich Böll, Saul Bellow, Raymond Chandler, and many more. From that time on, no matter what was happening around me, I could always find refuge in my work, in a world that was, at least partly, of my own creation.

At first my translations appeared under the name Pavel Kovaly; then, under the names Pavel and Heda Kovaly; finally, after 1963, I was permitted to publish under my own name. We still did not live in an apartment of our own and our lives were anything but easy, yet both of us were working and, gradually, people had stopped avoiding us.

The Czechoslovak Communist Party managed to evade the issue of the trials throughout the decade of the 1950s and into the early 1960s. What ended that era was not domestic discontent, which it could afford to ignore, but growing pressure from abroad. In Hungary, in Bulgaria, in Poland, the victims of the various "show trials," as they were now called, had been exonerated long before. It was only in our country that nothing rippled the surface of the muddy pond. Finally, in the spring of 1963, after seven years of stalling and fencing, the Party decided to admit that the Soviet Union had been its model for the execution and torture of innocent people, just as it had been its model for everything else.

The Central Committee prepared a document, titled "A Communication," which was made available only to Party members and which was read behind closed doors at meetings of all the Party organizations. The document conceded that all the people who had been convicted at the trials were innocent, that their confessions had been extorted by illegal means, and that during the interrogations a range of brutal and inhuman procedures had been used. The victims had been subjected to drugs as well as to physical and psychological torture.

The document also pronounced most of those who had been sentenced to death, including Rudolf Margolius, as fully rehabilitated in the view of the courts as well as in the eyes of the Party.

Only carefully selected Party officials were permitted to see the text of the document, and those Party members to whom it was read were strictly forbidden to discuss it. Despite that prohibition, I heard almost all of it verbatim by the following day. For me it meant, above all, that the time had come to address the most difficult issue of all—how to tell my son the truth about his father.

For years, Ivan knew nothing more than the fact that his father had died. My friends had argued all along that I should tell him everything. One should never lie to children, they said. When he finally finds out what happened, he'll turn against you; he'll never forgive you. Still I had decided to risk it. Better that he would hate me, I thought, than grow up hating the whole world, living with such incomprehensible injustice, always aware of being branded and excluded. There had, of course, always been the danger that a stranger would tell him or drop a hint, but the isolation in which we lived had protected him. We saw only a few friends, who had been careful to shield him.

I had, with great reluctance, carried out Rudolf's last wish and

167

changed Ivan's family name before he started school. Thanks to our changes of residence, Ivan's new schoolmates and their parents knew nothing about us.

Just before Easter, I thought again about telling him. He had a few days of vacation, which would give him some time to recover before going back to school.

One evening, I sat down with Ivan, my heart throbbing. But there was no way out. He was fifteen, almost an adult now; he would be able to take it. I told him everything I could, as honestly as I knew how. He listened in silence without looking at me, his head sinking lower and lower down over the table where we were sitting. He did not ask a single question. I knew I was smashing his world to bits, but I could spare him nothing, protect him from nothing.

The next few days were hard. Ivan kept his silence and avoided me.

Then one day he came to me of his own accord and said, "So Father really died for his convictions, didn't he?" Then he began to ask questions.

A load fell off my heart. The worst was behind us.

In mid-April of 1963, I received a summons to appear before the Central Committee. I spent the whole night before trying to choose the most effective course of action. I knew that they could not arrest me now, no matter what I might say, but I decided that the situation demanded dignity and an icy calm.

It did not turn out that way. The cowardice, the hypocrisy, the dishonesty, the shabbiness with which the Party officials tried to gloss over the past—all that could not be faced with calm and dignity. Hundreds of people had been murdered "for the good of the Party." Innocent people had been forced to confess to crimes they had never committed. And now those very people who had administered the torture and who had used the most contemptible methods of breaking people down were, once again, invoking "the good of the Party" to avoid admitting their own responsibility and guilt.

The Party had ordered the victims of the political purges to sacrifice their lives. Now it was ordering the executioners to cover up their crimes and hold on to their privileged positions.

It is astounding how terrified such men of action are of words. No act is too sordid for them to carry out, no act disturbs their sleep, so long as it is not called by its proper name, so long as it is not put into words. In this lies the great power of words, which are the only weapon of the defenseless.

The whole Central Committee building danced before my eyes as I walked in. After a short wait, I was ushered into an office where two comrades, utterly insignificant Party bureaucrats, were expecting me. I remember only one of them, a man named Jerman, who had gained a certain notoriety in the fifties by publishing a pamphlet in which he analyzed the depravity of the criminals associated with Slansky. Apparently Jerman had been selected to deal with the survivors because he had such command of the issues surrounding the trials.

"Who am I supposed to speak to here?" I said. "Take me to see the secretary general of the Central Committee."

"The Party entrusted *us* to go over the whole matter with you," Comrade Jerman replied pompously. "We will, of course, forward any comments you may have to the proper authorities."

"But *I'm* not willing to chat with just anyone," I said. "I consider that the case of Rudolf Margolius is important enough to be dealt with by the highest representative of the Party."

"Don't worry. Every word you tell us will be heard by the Comrade General Secretary."

That, I felt sure, was true. I knew that there had to be a recording device hidden somewhere in the room, taking down every word that was spoken. I haggled with them for a while longer but, eventually, I had to give up. It was clear that Comrade Novotny had no intention of risking a confrontation with one of his victims.

"All right," I said. "I see that I'll have to make do with you."

Comrade Jerman pulled a printed brochure from one of his desk drawers and, in a solemn, official tone, began to speak.

"In accordance with the instructions of the Party, we shall now read to you a communication which has been brought to the attention of all members of the . . ."

"Don't bother," I interrupted. "I know it by heart."

"But that's not possible!" Both comrades panicked. "This is a top-secret document! Who betrayed it to you?"

"How dare you ask me that question! Do you think everybody is an informer?"

That was the end of my icy calm and dignity. The two comrades

170

sat behind their table pale, in shock, only occasionally able to get in a word or two as I let them know exactly what I thought of the Party, its policies, and the intelligence and character of its representatives.

"But we had no way of knowing these people were innocent!"

"How could people who had been working with them for years not have known it? How could the Party not have known it when their confessions had been prepared ahead of time? There was a whole team of experts involved wasn't there? Why didn't Rudolf's boss stand up for him? Where was Minister Gregor? He knew for a *fact* that all the accusations against my husband were untrue!"

"Try to understand," Jerman stuttered. "He—he, too, was scared."

"What did a member of the government of a presumably sovereign state have to be afraid of? Of truth? Of responsibility? Why then wasn't he afraid of his conscience? And what about Bacilek who put on such a big show, promising my husband that he'd take care of me and my son, just to get him to accept the sentence quietly? Then he did everything he could to destroy us! To lie like that to a man who was going to die in a few hours! How could anyone be such a monster!"

I slammed my fist on the table so hard that everything jumped, including the two Party representatives. I raged until I ran out of breath, at which point Comrade Jerman seized the moment to say, "Please calm yourself. I have a document here issued for the exclusive use of the Central Committee. I was instructed to let you read the passage concerning your husband."

He pulled out of his drawer a fat volume, opened it to a premarked place, and let me read a single paragraph.

"The innocence of Rudolf Margolius has been established beyond a shadow of doubt. He did not in any way harm the interests of the State. On the contrary, a thorough review of his case has concluded that he fulfilled his duties in an exemplary manner. Had his proposals and plans been implemented, our national economy would have reaped considerable benefits."

Comrade Jerman looked beseechingly at me. Surely such a generous retraction would soften my heart. The Party had admitted its error; what more could I ask for?

"There's no point discussing with you what you'll never understand," I said. "Just tell me what guarantee exists that this won't happen again?"

"How can you even think of such a thing? Nothing like this can ever happen again! The collective leadership of the Party itself guarantees . . ."

"Oh please! Skip it and listen to me now. I demand a retrial of my husband's case. I want the accusations investigated, *in detail,* and I want them publicly refuted one by one. I want a public investigation into the methods by which his confession was obtained. On whose orders was it done, and by whom."

"Out of the question! The Party has already decided against individual retrials. The verdicts have been nullified for the entire group!" That meant a total cover-up.

"Will what you read to me be made public?"

"Out of the question! The Party has decided to handle the whole affair internally. Nothing will be made public."

"How can you imagine you can do that? During the trials you made enough noise to bring the world down, and now you want to hush up the rehabilitations? Don't you think people should know the truth? Is my child supposed to live out his life as the son of a criminal?"

"But of course not! Don't worry about it," said the Party representative soothingly. "You know how it is. Sooner or later the word gets around . . ."

There it was again—the old desperate sense of helplessness.

"Then give me a letter at least," I said. "On official stationary with the letterhead and the seal of the Central Committee. An official affidavit which my son can use to prove that his father is fully exonerated."

"We can't do that."

I started screaming again but I knew it was in vain. At last, I stood up to leave.

"You can keep your rehabilitation," I said. "The truth will come out. Just wait, you can't prevent it. And then you'll have to account for this too. I've waited eleven years. I can wait a few more."

They stood there, the two of them, dull, immobile, hard, and pale, like a couple of caryatides encrusted with pigeon droppings.

Comrade Jerman said, "I don't understand you. The other widows all came here and thanked us . . ."

I spun around and walked out of the room, slamming the door with a bang that resounded down the long corridor. Then I ran all the way to the nearest tavern, where Pavel was waiting and plotting an assault on the Central Committee building in the event that I did not return soon.

The next invitation I received was from a Dr. Bocek, the chairman of the Attorney's Association, who had been charged with the legal aspects of rehabilitating the victims of the Slansky trials. I went to see him expecting the same kind of farce that the comrades of the Central Committee had played out with me. But this time it was different. It did not take me long to realize that I was talking with an honest lawyer, who was trying, within the narrow limits of our crippled legal system, to enforce the law and to serve justice.

If Dr. Bocek had been given a free hand, the entire truth would have come out then. As it was, he had to wait five years until 1968, when, as Chief Justice of the Supreme Court, he ruled on the genuine rehabilitation of many who had been unjustly sentenced. In 1963, though, his efforts brought him the disapproval of the Party and cost him his job. He was the only honorable man among all the officials with whom I dealt at the time.

When I returned home from his office, I decided to make one more appeal. I wrote a formal complaint to the Prosecutor General.

"I request that legal action be taken against all those implicated in the death of Dr. Rudolf Margolius, executed on December 3, 1952, because I am convinced they knew that they were sending an innocent man to death. This knowledge makes them guilty of murder."

Among the people included in the designation "all those implicated" were almost all the members of the Central Committee starting with President of the Republic and Secretary General of the Party Comrade Antonin Novotny. Once again, friends warned me to be careful while crossing the street, but these were unnecessary fears. The comrades had no intention of paying attention to such a solitary voice, and the Prosecutor General, though bound by law to investigate all complaints and to file a report on his findings, did not even bother to acknowledge receipt of my letter.

I made my last official visit to the Ministry of Justice at the invitation of Deputy Minister Comrade Cihal. His letter to me had read something like this: Report to the Ministry of Justice for a hearing on the losses you sustained as a result of the arrest and conviction of Rudolf Margolius.

Comrade Cihal's reputation made the very idea of a serious hearing ludicrous, but I did not want to waste the opportunity.

I sat down at my typewriter and typed up a list.

> Summary of losses suffered by myself and my son due to the arrest and conviction of Dr. Rudolf Margolius
> - Loss of Father
> - Loss of Husband
> - Loss of Honor
> - Loss of Health
> - Loss of Employment and Opportunity to Complete Education
> - Loss of Faith in the Party and in Justice

There were some ten items on my list. Only at the end did I write

> - Loss of property

I dressed in my best clothes and borrowed two gold bracelets from a friend. I did not want the comrades to think they were rescuing some destitute wretch who would be grateful for their largesse.

174

Aside from Comrade Cihal, there were two other men sitting in the office—a representative from the Ministry of Social Welfare and, I think, a representative from the Ministry of Finance. All three were wearing carefully composed expressions of concern and sympathy, which were beginning to fray around the edges. Clearly, their effort to look like responsible officials was tiring them out.

"My dear lady," Cihal opened the proceeding. "We have invited you here to discuss the losses that . . ."

"Here you have a summary of my losses. I prepared it in writing."

Cihal took the list from me and, before he had read it to the end, became as red as a boiled lobster.

"I beg your pardon," he said with a huff. "You must understand that no one can make up these losses to you."

"Exactly," I said. "That's exactly why I wrote them up for you. So that you know that whatever you do, you can never undo what you have done."

"Look here," said the representative from the Ministry of Social Welfare, in a conciliatory tone. "We want to help you, award you compensation for lost property. After all, you lived in misery for years . . ."

"You murdered my husband. You threw me out of every job I had. You had me thrown out of a hospital! You threw us out of our apartment and into a hovel where only by some miracle we did not die. You ruined my son's childhood! And now you think you can compensate for that with a few crowns? That you can buy me off? Keep me quiet?"

With great satisfaction I watched the same ashen color spread across their official countenances as I had seen spread across the faces of the comrades at the Central Committee. The representative from the Ministry of Social Welfare, however, tried again.

"It's obvious that you're tired," he said. "Upset. That's understandable. Look, what if you went off somewhere for a vacation? To the seashore maybe? We would pay for it. You understand, it's not that we want to do you any favors . . ."

I jumped up from my chair.

175

"*You?* Do *me* favors? How dare you? I'm the one who would be doing you a favor if I decided to accept anything from you at all!"

I swept out of the office, leaving the comrades sitting at their table staring after me. I later learned that Cihal had called Dr. Bocek right after I left and had remonstrated with him for not having warned him about me. Bocek was ordered to make sure that I would never again appear in Cihal's office. It was fortunate for me that, at the time, no one could afford to arrest the widow of Rudolf Margolius.

As I walked out of the Ministry, I had an idea. I jumped onto the first streetcar, took it to the State Travel Office, and signed up for a trip to Bulgaria, to the coast of the Black Sea. I had to borrow the money to pay for the trip, but it was a beautiful vacation. Ivan, who had been depressed and troubled, swam in salt water for the first time, got tanned, and perked up. Every evening we would sit together on a café terrace above the sea watching the albatrosses flying away from the shore and later on, the silvery path that the moon traced on the water. We fell asleep to the quiet sound of the water sprinklers that showered the lawns and flowers in the garden below our windows.

Some time in June, the Party finally decided to publish a small notice in the newspapers to the effect that the men who received the death sentence in the Slansky trials had all been rehabilitated. Not one word more.

The comrades at the Ministry of Justice were instructed to limit the financial compensation to the next of kin strictly to the value of the confiscated property at the lowest possible estimate of its worth. From this estimate, a substantial sum was deducted to reflect the depreciation which this property would have suffered had it been in use over the years since it had been impounded.

Comrade Cihal won a special citation from the Party because he managed to pay out the absolute minimum to the widows of the convicted, many of whom were old and ill, and was thus able to return to the State Treasury a considerable part of the funds that had been allotted for restitution.

Three ministers were demoted as a result of the reassessment of the trials. Two of the most notorious torturers from the Ruzyn prison were given short prison sentences. One year later, they were granted amnesty and placed in good, well-paying jobs.

F or me, the Prague Spring of 1968 began late in 1967 when I saw posters on the street announcing a public lecture on crime in Czechoslovakia. It was to be held at the Slavic House, a large hall, where a panel of legal experts would answer questions from the floor. I had the evening free and decided to go.

The panel proved to be a mixed bag. Sitting up on the stage were Dr. Bocek, Comrade Cihal, an officer from the legal department of the army, and a few lawyers whom I did not know. The hall was filled with ordinary people, mostly middle-aged, the kind of people I saw every day in the street. I found a seat near the exit beside Rosemary Kavan, thinking that I would slip out at the first opportunity.

There was a brief general introduction about the rise in the crime rate among young people, and then the audience was invited to pose questions from the floor.

An older man who looked like a factory worker stood up.

"All this is very interesting," he said. "But I want to hear what really happened to all those people who were hanged in the fifties. For eleven years all the papers called them names and said they were the worst kind of criminals. Now we're told, just by the way, that they were all innocent. And that's that.

"You should explain to us here what kind of laws and courts

we have when innocent people get hanged. And why aren't we told what really happened so that we don't have to feel like idiots or scoundrels for having agreed with it? When they send a convicted spy to prison somewhere in the West, we organize protest rallies. Here at home we let our own people get hanged and even pass resolutions to approve it! How do you think we feel now?"

That was only the beginning. Questions and shouts rained down on the panel from all corners of the hall. Some of the gentlemen seated onstage began to wipe their foreheads. At first, I could hardly believe it. I thought that everyone had forgotten the trials long before. It had been sixteen years! And these were ordinary people, the sort of people I had thought never showed an interest in anything except their own well-being.

It was at this meeting that I first became aware of the spontaneous solidarity of the decent which had started to grow and which reached its climax when the Russians invaded Czechoslovakia. As soon as the questions started, my friend Rosemary who was working as a reporter for an English-language magazine published in Prague, began taking notes. I tried to help her. About half an hour into the questions, a young man in the balcony who had a good view of the hall raised his hand.

"Watch what you say folks!" he called out. "There're two informers sitting among us. I can see them very well from up here and they're writing down everything anyone says!"

Rosemary and I looked up and, from the stage, Bocek started laughing. Only then did we realize that the young man was talking about us.

"Don't worry friends," Bocek said. "You have nothing to be afraid of from those two!"

The young man understood, gave us a conspiratorial nod, and the whole hall burst out laughing.

Bocek then gave a factual, cogent summary of the trials and their aftermath. Cihal slouched deeper into his chair, and later slunk away like a whipped dog. It was typical of the prevailing mood that no one attacked or even threatened him. People seemed to understand that violence and revenge, no matter how justifiable, could not be part of the rebirth we were just beginning to experience, of the short but unforgettable rebirth that became known as the Prague Spring.

That same spirit of tolerance prevailed at all subsequent rallies, meetings, and discussions. Whenever someone dared to stand up in defense of the old order, people heard him out, with contempt perhaps but also with patience, and then repudiated his arguments and paid him no more attention. On one of these occasions I remember a distraught bureaucrat who lost all control and screamed at the top of his lungs, "What do you want? I've been a Party hack all my life so what do you want me to do now? Look for a job? Work?"

I shall never forget the first large youth rally that March. Some twenty thousand students and young workers jammed into the main exhibition hall, thousands more were packed into adjoining halls, and more gathered outside, where confused and surly policemen tried in vain to provoke some incident that would give them a pretext to break up the meeting.

All these young people had been born and reared in a society walled in by censorship, where the expression of any independent opinion was routinely treated as a crime. What could they know about democracy? How could they even know what they wanted? But as the evening progressed, those of us who were much older grew ever more amazed and impressed. We were taken not only by the precision and clarity of the ideas that were voiced but by the high level of the discussion and the discipline of that mass of young people. They knew exactly what they wanted and what they did not want, what was open for compromise and what they refused to give up.

The spring of 1968 had all the intensity, anxiety and unreality of a dream come true. People flooded the narrow streets of Prague's Old Town and the courtyards of Hradcany Castle and stayed out long into the night. If anyone set out for a walk alone, he would soon join a group of others to chat or tell a joke, and we all would listen with relief as the ancient walls echoed with the sound of laughter. Even long after the Castle gates closed, people would

180

remain standing on the ramparts looking down at the flickering lights of a city that could not sleep for happiness.

Every morning on the staircase of the once-dreaded Central Committee building, women would wait for Alexander Dubcek, the new Secretary General, to arrive at his office. They brought pieces of homemade cake or bunches of flowers. Children gave him their teddy bears for good luck. No one missed a chance to see him on television. It was rare joy to watch a Party official who would sometimes stutter and whose glasses kept sliding down his nose.

The day President of the Republic Antonin Novotny had resigned, in January, I had gone shopping for groceries. The store had been crowded with hurried, impatient people as usual but, for the first time I could remember, no one was pushing or arguing. The girl who was standing in front of me on line turned around and said, "Look! Everyone's smiling today!"

Late one evening, I was returning home from a meeting at Strahov Library, high above Prague, with a woman friend. It was cold and, as we ran down the steep slope of Neruda Street, we decided to stop in at a little wine cellar to warm up.

The place was packed. All public places were packed then as if, after all those years of isolation, people could not get enough of one another's company. We could not find a place to sit down and were about to leave when two young men at a nearby table got up.

"You don't want to go out into that cold again—you look frozen," one of them said. "Take our seats. We've stayed long enough."

We sat down at a small table that was already accomodating six people. They immediately began signalling the waiter to bring us some hot mulled wine.

My friend, whose husband had spent six years in jail and had died shortly after his release, said to me, "We've paid an outrageous price for this, but if it lasts, I want to make peace with the past. Not forgive. Not forget. But come to terms with it. I never imagined that life could be so magnificent, that people could feel so strongly that they belong together, that their life has a meaning.

Just look around! You see the same joy on every face, the same happiness . . ."

". . . and the same fear that they'll lose it all," said the stranger sitting next to me, and smiled.

Groups of students would sit around the Jan Hus monument in the Old Town Square playing their guitars and singing till dawn. Tourists from abroad and our own people would join them, listening, and pondering those beautiful, deceitful words carved into the stone: Truth Prevails.

Does it? Truth alone does not prevail. When it clashes with power, truth often loses. It prevails only when people are strong enough to defend it.

We worried constantly that the Soviets would not tolerate our outburst of independence. For them, freedom was a virulent disease which could spread to other parts of their sphere of influence before they were able to wipe it out. They had crushed the liberation movements in Hungary, in Poland, in East Germany. What chance did we have?

In July, the leaders of the Soviet Union, East Germany, Poland, Hungary and Bulgaria met in Warsaw and sent a note to Prague. It was full of threats denouncing our leadership as well as the "situation" in Czechoslovakia which jeopardized the "vital interests of all Socialist countries." Shortly afterward a meeting of the members of the Soviet Politburo and the Czechoslovak Presidium was scheduled to take place in the village of Cierna to discuss these issues. It was hoped that a solution acceptable to both sides would be found.

Nobody slept the night before our delegation was due to go to Cierna. The streets were crowded, as though it were broad daylight, and people clasped hands and called out encouragements to one another. Everyone knew our independence was at stake. The next day, a printed declaration appeared on little tables on street corners and in arcades. People by the thousands stopped to sign their names to this declaration of loyalty to a socialism that did not murder or intimidate or lie, to a socialism that did not bestow social equality and economic security upon those who were willing

182

to silence their consciences and to renounce human dignity. This was the socialism that Rudolf had sought. Twenty years before, it had been an illusion; now it was becoming a reality. The declaration ended with the words: "We shall not retreat, so long as we live, from this road we have chosen."

I signed it twice, once for myself and once for my son.

Ivan was already living in London. After the truth about his father's death had sunk in, he felt he could not remain in a country where such atrocities were silently tolerated. I agreed. All Ivan's relatives, both maternal and paternal, had been murdered by barbarians who had invaded our country. Not one member of his family had died a natural death. There was no peace and no future in the heart of Europe. After finishing high school, Ivan had managed to escape to England and, under Dubcek, I had no difficulty visiting him there. I was planning another trip for the end of that summer.

Now, as I signed the declaration, I thought to myself: I really mean it this time, Rudolf. This was your dream and, if we realize it, you will not have died in vain.

The negotiations in Cierna dragged on and on, and public anxiety about the proceedings intensified every day. Any scrap of news made the rounds of Prague within hours. Mountains of petitions, tons of paper were flown in to Cierna. There were expressions of confidence in our delegation and hope that our representatives would not yield to pressure, would take strength from this well of support from the people at home.

Cierna is a tiny town situated almost directly on the border between Czechoslovakia and the Soviet Union. From its streets one could see the Soviet Army units massed on the Russian side. The negotiations were conducted in special railway cars, and the Soviet delegation had its train taken back across the border every night.

Rumors were rife. I heard that once, when the negotiations had come to a halt, Dubcek had gone alone into the Russian train to have a private word with Brezhnev. The villagers dropped whatever they were doing and gathered at the railway station, standing silently on the tracks behind the Russian train: If you take him away and with him our freedom, it will be over our dead bodies.

The negotiations ended in a compromise. Under intense pressure from the Soviets, our representatives agreed to rein in those aspects of liberalization which most offended Moscow. The Soviets agreed to refrain from interference in our domestic matters. This agreement was immediately confirmed and signed at a conference in Bratislava.

The joint declaration satisfied no one but we were all so exhausted by the build-up of tension that we decided to hope for the best. They will try to push us as far as they can, we told each other. Maybe we will have to give in here and there but at least the danger of armed intervention has been averted. Shortly after our delegation returned to Prague, the Soviet troops that had been conducting maneuvers in Czechoslovakia since that spring left our territory. For the moment, everything was all right we thought. People sighed with relief and took the vacations they had been postponing for months.

At daybreak on August 21, a friend of mine was sitting by a pond fishing. The bait was in the water, the mist was rising, and the birds began to chirp. He made himself comfortable, took out a thick slice of bread and butter, and turned on his transistor radio. He listened for a while, shook his head, listened again. What kind of peculiar broadcast was this? He stuck the rest of the bread into his pocket, secured the fishing rod with a couple of stones, and returned slowly to his cabin where his wife was still sleeping. He sat down at the edge of the bed and shook her.

"Helena, wake up! They're broadcasting the strangest play. Something about the Russians invading us."

His wife yawned, sat up, listened. Then she screamed, "You fool! It's true! Occupation!"

At about that same time I was already behind the wheel of my tiny Fiat, breaking all speed limits between Prague and the Austrian border. The telephone had rung in my apartment at four that morning.

"Heda, the Russians have crossed our borders. Prague is being invaded by airborne troops. Call all your friends. Let them know before they go out."

I gripped the telephone receiver with both hands. "No. No, it can't be true," I moaned. "It's a lie."

"It's true," said the tired voice. "It would be a hideous lie. But it's an even more hideous truth."

I stood by the telephone for a while, my mind a blank. Then I dialed the police. An agitated voice answered after the first ring.

"Is it true?" I asked.

"Turn on your radio."

I bounded over to the radio.

"The armies of five powers have crossed the Czechoslovak frontiers . . ."

I returned to the telephone and dialed one number after another. At the other end of the line one voice after another cried out, "No. No . . ."

At that hour, all of Prague's telephones must have been ringing.

I was at home alone. My husband was on a lecture tour in the United States. My son was in England. I thought: As soon as the Russians reach the western borders, they will close them. It will be just like the 1950s. I will never see my son again.

I grabbed a small bag, threw in a few necessities and, half an hour later, I was speeding away. Today I cannot recall anything of that 160-mile drive except that, long before I reached the border, it was broad daylight, and, as I neared it, I saw a large sign which warned that entry into the border zone without a valid exit permit was strictly forbidden.

That, of course, was awkward. I had no exit permit. I turned the car around and parked it a few hundred feet back. Then I took my bag and, as casually as possible, strolled into the woods.

They caught me about twenty minutes later. The border zone was several miles wide; the forest was sparse and offered little cover. Two border guards appeared between the trees, ordered me to halt, and then escorted me back to the road. There they put me in their jeep and drove me back to my car. One of them got in beside me and ordered me to drive to the nearest village where there was a border guard outpost complete with a small jail. A rather disturbed-looking man was just being led into it.

The station was manned by a few guards and their young commander, all as upset as myself. I told them who I was and a violent argument ensued: the name Margolius was enough to provoke instant reaction.

But the commander stood by his obligations.

"Please understand," he said. "I'm a soldier. I have my orders. I really should arrest you for breaking the law. Instead I'm only asking you to return home. Should I receive orders to let people out, I'll do it with pleasure but, for the time being, it's impossible. You must understand that if I disobey one order, I can't be relied upon to obey other orders—for instance, the order to resist the enemy."

For a time we kept arguing, trying to sort out our thoughts, trying to confront together a situation which was too enormous for us to comprehend. Suddenly I realized that this would not be an easy triumph for an arrogant superpower. We would not surrender without a fight. In the end, the young men all solemnly promised to keep faith with their country and to accept orders from no one but their supreme commander, President Svoboda, and I agreed to return to Prague.

The officer accompanied me back to my car and asked, "Aren't you afraid to go back alone? I could send someone with you."

I thanked him, but said I did not feel that any of us were alone now.

The next day the border guards relaxed their surveillance and thousands of people left the country without exit permits. But by that time I was no longer thinking of leaving. The thrill of the struggle had engulfed me.

As I drove back to Prague that morning through the landscape of lakes and deep forests, I picked up three soldiers who had been home on leave. They kept urging me to drive faster so that they could rejoin their units and fight the invaders. But the order to fire never came.

All the towns through which we passed were already covered

186

with posters and proclamations. Local radio stations were broadcasting nonstop, barricades had begun to rise in some places, and in others people with clenched fists lined the streets.

I got back to Prague shortly after noon. I had to make detours through side streets because tanks were stationed in the major intersections, blocking off the main avenues to traffic. Crowds of people surrounded those tanks, trying to communicate with the soldiers in broken Russian.

"What's your business here?" I heard someone ask. "Do you even know where you are?"

"In Germany," grunted a soldier.

"Don't you have eyes? Can't you see you're in Prague?"

The soldier sneered and turned away.

Just as I started my car again, I saw a blonde girl dance up to the rear of that tank and toss a flaming torch under it.

At the next intersection another young woman dashed up to my car window and threw in a bag of tricolor ribbons—the colors of the Czechoslovak flag—and pamphlets with the instruction: "Distribute them!"

After that, I stopped at every corner. People crowded around my car, tore the pamphlets from my hands, pinned the tricolor onto their lapels. At every stop, someone would stick another poster or flag onto my car and, before long, it was completely covered with slogans: Murderers Go Home! Death to the Invaders! Bring Back Dubcek! Words. Words against tanks. Fourteen million people tried to defend their freedom with their bare hands while bloodied flags covered our first dead.

At Wenceslas Square at the center of Prague, below the bullet-scarred facade of the National Museum, tens of thousands of people with transistors to their ears milled around in streets filled with crushed automobiles and pieces of masonry that had been shot down from the surrounding buildings. Walls were covered with painted slogans. Trucks draped with Czechoslovak flags rammed into the Russian tanks and the air rang with the sound of intermittant gunfire.

Standing in the crowd, I felt that this was the supreme moment of our lives. During the night of the invasion, when we lost everything, we found something that people in our world hardly dare to hope for: ourselves and each other. In all those faces, in all those eyes, I saw that we all thought and felt alike, that we all strove for the same things.

Prague resisted in every way it could. Street signs disappeared or were turned around so that the invaders were unable to find their way through the city. License plate numbers of Soviet Security cars were painted in large digits on the walls. Radio and, later, television broadcasts were transmitted from makeshift facilities that were moved from place to place, eluding the Russians. At the same time, the train carrying Russian radio station-detector equipment was lost on its way to Prague. For days it was shunted from siding to siding by Czechoslovak railwaymen. And throughout the city, hungry Russian soldiers who could not get a crumb of food or glass of water from the population wandered through streets where all the traffic signs pointed in one direction: back to Moscow.

On the third day of the invasion, I happened to hear the broadcast of a radio station from a town on our border with East Germany, appealing for volunteers who spoke German and other foreign languages, and who could transmit our news abroad. I called a journalist friend, Jirka, and asked, "Are you coming?"

The Russians stopped us three times to search the car but did not find the stacks of pamphlets I had hidden under my seat and which we passed out along our route. In one of the small towns on the way we were surrounded by a group of young people on motorbikes who were patrolling the roads. They had organized the entire district and were able immediately to identify any stranger or strange vehicle that entered the area. Even old people helped. Grandfathers in wheelchairs sat at intersections, signalling to us with their canes, indicating the proximity of the enemy and directing us to make detours. In one village an old invalid directed traffic with his crutches.

The young patrolmen persuaded us to stay in their town. They took us to their local National Committee where a new chairman, a smart, good-humored stocky fellow, was trying to cope with the situation as well as he could. My mind skipped back over my dismal dealings with various local National Committees of the past. Where had all the bureaucrats gone?

The chairman put us to work right away. We broadcast over the town's public address system instructions for the population and bulletins about the movement of troops in the neighborhood. We wrote leaflets and newsletters which the young men on the motorbikes promptly distributed throughout the district. But units of the Polish occupation army were approaching and the mood of the community was grim.

When the first troops entered the town, their commander sent word that he wished to negotiate with the National Committee. Embarrassed, the chairman scratched his head. "How are we going to talk to them? Does anyone speak Polish?"

I found I still had long-rusted scraps of Polish that I had picked up in the concentration camps some twenty-five years earlier.

"If no one else does," I said, "I think I can manage."

The Polish delegation was made up of a perfumed colonel in dress uniform, a sweaty major in rolled-up shirt-sleeves, and an adjutant who did not once open his mouth during the proceedings. We sat at a table—the three Poles on one side; four Czechs and myself on the other. The confrontation was icy.

The Colonel began.

"First of all, I wish to emphasize that we have not come to interfere in your internal affairs. But you have allowed your Party to slip into the hands of right wing opportunists, Zionists even, the kind of people we in Poland have managed to eradicate . . ."

I translated in the juiciest terms I could find.

"If you didn't come here to interfere in our internal affairs, then what is it you're doing here?" asked the chairman. "Tell us what you want and cut the preaching."

"We need water," said the Colonel. "For the troops and for the trucks. Order your people to give us access to their wells and to let us draw as much water as we need."

The chairman threw up his hands. "I wish I could," he said. "I know those soldiers must be thirsty and you can't move your trucks without water. But unfortunately this is a dry area. We don't have a drop of water to spare. Sorry.

"Now listen to our demand: we ask you to clear the road where you've halted your troops. It's the only road linking several communities and we need it cleared for deliveries of food."

The major pulled out a map. "Impossible," he said. "This is a strategic location."

"Out of the question," added the Colonel. "Not open to negotiation. Give us the water."

"We have no water," I translated. "Clear our highway."

It went around in circles like that until there was no longer any need for me to translate.

"You know what?" the Colonel said finally. "Give us the water. Then we'll discuss your request with the rest of our comrades and inform you of our decision."

"Clear the road," said the chairman. "Then we'll discuss your request with the rest of our comrades and inform you of our decision."

Everyone stood up. On one side, the polished, arrogant soldiers of an occupying army; on the other, the plain, shrewd Czech villagers. How many times in Czech history have we acted out a similar confrontation?

We won that skirmish. But, of course, it made little difference. The real battle was taking place in Moscow, where our leaders who had been kidnapped by the Soviets on the first day of the occupation were being held and subjected to all kinds of insults, threats, and other forms of maltreatment. They tried desperately to negotiate the withdrawal of the occupation armies with Brezhnev and his associates, knowing that if they were not able to hold their own, any small domestic victory would be turned against us. We would be made to pay dearly for it.

Finally on the evening of the seventh day, the voice of Dubcek, the only man we trusted, came over the radio. It was a voice heavy with helplessness and defeat. We listened to the long pauses between his words and the barely audible sighs that told us more than the words. Darkness was settling over the lovely countryside, the homeland of despair, as I drove back to Prague. Someone had whitewashed a few words onto a fence near my street.

"Dearest Dubcek," they read. "We understand."

There is little to add.

Rudolf's path, that I had sworn not to abandon, now led to the border. But I still could not make the decision to leave. I walked around Prague for weeks, talking to friends and strangers alike, trying to persuade myself that no one would forget and that the future would not be submission, but waiting for another opportunity. I could see that one important change had already occurred—the spell under which the Soviets had held many die-hard true believers was broken for good. There would be no more illusions, no more self-deception about the nature of Big Brother. The grim reign of ideology was over, and maybe truth in its own oblique, unpredictable way had prevailed after all.

At the end of September, the invaders were still sitting in full strength at the airports. I boarded a train, carrying two small suitcases and twenty dollars in my pocket.

The train was crammed. Facing me sat two students, a young man and a girl, who were headed for Holland. We talked about books and about life, and the pretty girl kept complaining that she had left behind her new hat.

"Don't you think," she kept asking, "that going into exile would be less awful if I were travelling in a beautiful new hat?"

Later, a grouchy middle-aged German tourist came into the compartment with her small daughter. The little girl stared at the three of us curiously and then asked, "Mutti, why are these people so sad?"

Her mother snapped at her. "Don't you know the Czechs love their country, you dummy!"

Just before we reached the forests at the border, the train stopped and stood on the tracks for a while. An ancient railway man hobbled past our car, waved his cane, and shouted gleefully up to us.

"We have a hospital full of Russians here! We didn't give them anything to eat and they went out to the woods to pick mushrooms and now they're all sick! Don't worry. We'll get them out of here yet!"

The train did not stop long at the border and, when it began to move, I leaned out the window as far as I could, looking back. The last thing I saw was a Russian soldier, standing guard with a fixed bayonet.